MW00678085

How To Get Top Dollar$ for your Workers' Compensation Claim

- 15 costly mistakes that will ruin your workers compensation claim

- How to get your payments on time

- What to do when your employer wants you back at work and you are not able to work

- 17 rules for dealing with vocational rehabilitation counselors

- How to handle job interviews

- Do you need a lawyer

- Can you change doctors

- How to keep them from stopping your benefits

- When should you settle

- Can you get paid when you was at fault

- What you should do immediately after your accident

- How long will you get paid

- How to deal with doctors

- When do you have to return to work

- 6 rules for dealing with workers comp nurses

- 9 qualifications your lawyer should have

- Can they switch doctors

- How do you file a claim

- What benefits are you entitled to receive

- How long can you go to the doctor

How To Get **TOP DOLLAR$**
for your

Workers'
Compensation
Claim

Brent Adams

Offices in:
Raleigh, Fayetteville and Dunn

1-800-INJURED
(1-800-465-8733)
1-800-849-5931
www.ncpersonalinjurylaw.com
brent@brentadams.com

Word Association Publishers
www.wordassociation.com

Copyright © 2008 by Brenton D. Adams

All rights reserved. No part of this book may be used or reproduced in any manner whatsoever without written permission of the author.

Printed in the United States of America.

ISBN: 978-1-59571-252-3

Library of Congress Control Number: 2008920781

Word Association Publishers

205 5th Avenue

Tarentum, PA 15084

www.wordassociation.com

TABLE OF CONTENTS

- Falls
- Horseplay
- Assaults At Work
- Storm And Weather Related Injuries
- Suicide
- The Accident Must Occur While At Work
- The Going And Coming Rule
- Accidents Which Occur Outside The State
2. Specific Traumatic Incident Resulting In A Hernia
   Or Back Injury
3. Occupational Diseases
   - Exposure To A Greater Risk Of Harm (A Catch-All Provision)
   - Silicosis And Asbestosis Are Treated Differently
   - Where Disease Results From An Accident

- The Accident Must Be Reported In Writing Quickly
- Claims Must Be Filed With The N.C. Industrial Commission
  Within Two Years

- What Is A Disability?
- Pre-Existing Conditions
- Proving Disability

- When Are Workers' Compensation Payments Due?
- There Is A Penalty For Late Payment
- Interest On Award Of Workers' Compensation Benefits
- Worker Gets Ten Percent Increase In Benefits If Employer
  Violates Safety Statute

- Violation Of Safety Standard By Employee
- Injured Employee Cannot Recover If His Injury Or Death Was Caused By
  His Intoxication Or By His Being Under The Influence Of Controlled
  Substances
- The Worker Intentionally Injures Himself

◆

BRENT ADAMS

Appendix

WE ARE NOT AFRAID
TO TAKE ON THE INSURANCE INDUSTRY.

We are different from your usual personal injury and workers' compensation law firm.

We do not operate a settlement mill.

Lawyers refer to law firms that take a large volume of cases and settle them cheaply without any intention to take the cases to trial as a "settlement mill."

We do not take just the easy cases and settle for whatever the insurance wants to pay for your claim. We know who the enemy is and we fight them tooth and nail to try hard to get the best results for our clients.

The insurance companies know us and know that we will not bow down to their ridiculously low offers. The insurance companies know which law firms will actually go to court and fight for their clients and which ones will not. Insurance companies will pay less when they know your lawyer will not go to court.

We know that it is far better to settle your case when the insurance company is willing to pay a fair amount. We are able to successfully settle the vast majority of our cases because the insurance companies know that we will take them to court if they are not fair with our clients. We know that it is better for you to settle your case quickly and we try very hard to do just that. We understand that it is your money and that you are entitled to receive it back from the insurance company as quickly as possible. We can do that successfully for you because the insurance companies know that if they do not make a reasonable offer to us to settle your case, we will take them to court. Fortunately, for this reason, we do not have to take many cases to court. But when we have to, we will go into court for our clients with our years of experience and the latest technology and do our best to obtain the highest recovery possible.

Since 1973, I have represented accident, injury and disability victims throughout the state of North Carolina. The vast majority of these cases are referred to us by former satisfied clients, as well as other lawyers. We currently have offices in Raleigh, Fayetteville, and Dunn. However, if we take your case, and your home is not convenient to one of our locations, we will come to you. We will not inconvenience you by requiring you to travel to us.

Over the years with a successful law practice, I have assembled a group of highly skilled lawyers who love to go to court to fight the insurance companies. All the lawyers in my offices share my zeal to do our very best to obtain for you the highest settlement possible. We do not accept all cases that are presented to us, however. We only take the meritorious cases, those cases in which we can be most effective for you. Sometimes, the best advice we can give our clients is that they have a case that no lawyer can win. If that is the assessment we make in your case, we will be honest and up front with you about that fact so that you will not waste your time and money on a case that cannot be won. This does not mean that we do not take on difficult cases. We take cases that many lawyers turn down when we see merit to the case that other lawyers miss.

Many times clients come to us with cases for which they are clearly entitled recovery. However, because the injuries to the claimant are relatively minor, we may determine there is nothing we can do to help the client. In those cases, the clients would be better off settling with the insurance company on their own and keeping all the money for themselves, rather than paying a lawyer a percentage of the recovery. We tell our clients up front if we do not feel we can recover for them a net recovery (after attorney's fees and other costs) larger than they can collect from the insurance company on their own. If this is the case, we will give you our special report which teaches you how to settle your case on your own without a lawyer. We will not take your case unless we feel we can put more money in your pocket than you could recover on your own.

If your case does, however, meet our requirements and we accept it, you can be assured that your case will receive my personal attention. I, along with selected lawyers on our staff, will aggressively represent you, communicate with you frequently on the progress of your case, and give you our honest advice as to whether you should settle your case or instruct us to go to trial for you. If we do accept your case, we will be willing to represent you on a contingency fee basis. Under this agreement, you pay us only a percentage of your total recovery. If, for some unexpected reason, there is no recovery, you will not owe us any attorney's fees. Most clients do not wish to hire us on an hourly basis; however, we are always willing to represent clients on an hourly basis. We will fully explain our fees and the anticipated cost to you before we start working on your case. We will enter into a written contract with you so that you will fully understand our fee agreement. This written contract protects you from "surprises" later on.

After an attorney-client relationship has been established between us, we will decide together, as a team the best tactics and methods to use in order to attempt to produce for you the highest recovery possible.

- Fighting insurance companies since 1973
- Former Vice-President of the North Carolina Academy of Trial Lawyers
- Member, Million Dollar Advocates Forum
- Board Certified by the National Board of Trial Advocacy
- Lectures to lawyers on trial practice at programs sponsored by the Association of Trial Lawyers of America, The North Carolina Academy of Trial Lawyers, The North Carolina Bar Association, Wake Forest University School of Law and the Melvin M. Belli Society
- Member, Board of Directors of the Southern Trial Lawyers Association.
- Former North Carolina State Delegate to the American Association for Justice, formerly the Association of Trial Lawyers of America.
- Author of Consumer Books and Reports on law related topics
- Former research assistant to an Associate Justice of the Supreme Court of North Carolina.
- Author of Legal Manuscripts published by the American Association for Justice (formerly the Association of Trial Lawyers of America), The North Carolina Bar Association, Wake Forest University School of Law and The Wake Forest Law Review.

PART I

Information You Need to Keep You From
Getting Ripped Off by Your Employer

SECTION A
DO NOT CONSIDER THIS BOOK TO BE LEGAL ADVICE

I know all of the tricks and tactics that employers and insurance companies will try to use against you – and so should you. Even before you were injured, the insurance industry had been fighting you by pushing for changes in the law which hurt you and your claim.

When you are injured, you enter into a combat zone. Your enemy is a well-funded employer and insurance company and their experienced lawyers who have fought these battles everyday for many years. You will not be alone in this battle, however. We will be by your side every step of the way.

North Carolina Bar rules, by which I am governed, however, will not allow me to give legal advice in this book. Here, we can offer you some guidance, inform you of what you can expect and caution you against various traps you may encounter on your journey towards achieving adequate compensation for your workers' compensation claim. Please do not construe anything in this book to be legal advice until you have agreed to hire us and we have agreed to accept your case.

SECTION B
WHO WROTE THIS BOOK AND WHY YOU SHOULD READ IT

Thank you for requesting this book. I have included information here that will help in your battle with your employer and its workers' compensation insurance company.

I wrote this book for victims of work-related injuries and diseases so that they could have good solid objective information before hiring an attorney or dealing with the employer or the insurance company. As I discuss in this book, a lawyer need not be hired in every workers' compensation case. There are some cases that are just so small that the victim would be better handling the case on his own without a lawyer. However, since the cards are stacked against the injured worker, I feel that you should have this valuable information now, for free, before you are pressured by your employer or its insurance adjuster to give them information and before you settle your case.

My name is Brent Adams and I have been representing individuals against employers and insurance companies since 1973. I limit my practice to workers' compensation, personal injury, disability cases, and claims against insurance companies. If you have a traffic ticket, want a divorce, need tax advice, or want an estate plan, I cannot help you. You can find more about me and my law firm at our website at *www.ncpersonalinjurylaw.com*.

- Fighting Insurance Companies since 1973
- Former Vice-President of the North Carolina Academy of Trial Lawyers
- Member, Million Dollar Advocates Forum

- Board Certified by the National Board of Trial Advocacy
- Lectures to lawyers on trial practice at programs sponsored by the American Association for Justice (formerly the Association of Trial Lawyers of America), The North Carolina Academy of Trial Lawyers, The North Carolina Bar Association, Wake Forest University School of Law and the Melvin M. Belli Society
- Member, Board of Directors of the Southern Trial Lawyers Association
- Former North Carolina State Delegate to the American Association for Justice, (formerly the Association of Trial Lawyers of America)
- Author of Consumer Books and Reports on law related topics
- Former research assistant to an Associate Justice of the Supreme Court of North Carolina
- Author of Legal Manuscripts published by the American Association of Justice (formerly the Association of Trial Lawyers of America), The North Carolina Bar Association, Wake Forest University School of Law and The Wake Forest Law Review.

Over the years I have experienced how unfairly work-related accident victims are treated by their employers and the insurance industry. I have developed a strong passion for fighting insurance companies to try to get the best result for our clients.

At this writing, we currently have seven attorneys on our staff who share my passion for representing injured, disabled, and hurting people. We do not represent insurance companies, banks, manufacturers, or other large corporations. Our clients are the ones who really matter, the people who toil and work to make our state and nation a better place. We represent injured workers throughout North Carolina with offices in Raleigh, Fayetteville, and Dunn. The lawyers at our offices are assisted by experienced paralegals, former claims adjusters, and legal secretaries. All of us share the same concern for our clients and work hard to give everyone who calls upon us our very best effort.

We recognize that being the victim of a work-related accident or disease is very traumatic not only for the victims but for their families as well. Not only are the victims in pain and out of work, they also have serious concerns for their ability to support their family in the future. Our lawyers and staff are easily accessible by phone or email, and personal visits to our office are welcome. We do not mind taking the time with our clients that is necessary to try to get them through this very difficult period. We pride ourselves on the personal attention that we give to all of our clients.

We have represented thousands of people who have been injured at work and people who have been injured outside the work environment as a result of negligence of others.

We have also represented families of deceased loved ones in wrongful death cases. North Carolina State Bar rules will not allow me to include here the specific amounts we have recovered for our clients through jury verdicts and settlements. While each case is different, and past results cannot be used to predict future success, I am proud to say that I have been privileged to help my clients and their families recover millions of dollars in settlements and verdicts from insurance companies. We do not promise, however, that we can obtain any specific result or injury for you in your case if you hire us.

SECTION C
WHY DID I WRITE THIS BOOK?

I want to level the playing field for victims of work-related accidents and occupational diseases. The deck is currently stacked heavily in favor of employers and their insurance companies. The insurance companies take advantage of people before they have had a chance to talk to a lawyer. Adjusters frequently appear on the doorstep of victims of work-related accidents and occupational diseases and pressure victims to settle their cases quickly before they even have a chance to finish treatment from their doctors or to obtain from their doctor an assessment of the true nature and extent of their injuries. The obvious reason insurance companies act so promptly when trying to settle cases is to try to take advantage of these unfortunate workers and settle their cases cheaply.

You may not need a lawyer to help you with your workers' compensation case but you should be armed with this important information from the beginning of your claim. I wrote this book so that you could be informed now before you make some important decisions about your case.

I am fed up with employers and insurance companies taking advantage of injured workers before they have a chance to talk to a lawyer.

Most lawyers will require you to sign a contract before they give you some of the information which I have provided for you here. I believe that you should have this information now without any pressure so that you have plenty of time to just think about what you should do and discuss it with your family. Hiring a lawyer to represent you is a very important decision that should not be taken lightly.

This book also serves the purposes of saving me time when I talk with you. We have included a large amount of information in this book, and it saves me the hours of time that it would take each day to talk to all of our potential clients who call. We do not accept every case that comes to us. Each year we turn down valid cases that do not meet our selection criteria. Rather than going over this information with you on the phone, by writing this book I am able to tell you what you need to know so that you can make an informed decision about what you should do to protect yourself and your case. Even if I do not take your case, I would like for you to be educated about the process so that you will not be victimized by your employer or its insurance company.

SECTION D
THE 15 COSTLY MISTAKES THAT COULD RUIN YOUR WORKERS' COMPENSATION CLAIM

1. Failure to Report the Claim to Your Employer.

North Carolina law requires that a claim be reported to your employer in writing within 30 days from the date of the injury. Although in most cases you could proceed with your claim even if you do not file a written report in 30 days, these reports should be filed in writing immediately. See Section 15.

2. Failure to File a Claim with the Industrial Commission.

North Carolina law requires that a claim be filed with the North Carolina Industrial Commission within two years from the date of the accident. In the case of occupational diseases, the claim must be filed within two years from the date the worker became unable to work. See Section 15. With respect to occupational diseases, the filing requirements vary.

3. Failure to Inform the Doctor of the Details of Your Accident.

If your medical records do not reflect the fact that you have been in an accident, your claim may be suspect. Insurance companies use any excuse they can find to deny your claim. The absence of any information about your accident in your medical records may give them the excuse they want. See Section N.

4. Failure to Keep a Job Search Log.

As the worker, you have the burden of proving that you are unable to work as a result of a workers' compensation injury or occupational disease. This is true even after you start receiving workers' compensation benefits. One of the best ways to prove that you cannot work is to show that you have honestly tried to work but were unable to find and maintain a job. A job search log is the best way to document your efforts to find a job. See Section 21.

5. Failure to Fully Inform Your Lawyer of All Facts.

Workers' compensation cases are difficult enough to handle successfully, even when a lawyer has all the facts. If you do not fully inform your lawyer concerning all facts, the good, the bad and the ugly, you severely handicap your lawyer's ability to win the case for you. Many facts which you may feel to be adverse, can be successfully handled. Do not short change yourself by keeping your lawyer in the dark.

6. Failure to Fully Cooperate with All Vocational Rehabilitation Efforts.

The point at which the insurance company hires a vocational rehabilitation specialist to actively become involved in trying to find a job for you is probably the most critical point in the claims process. You should not attempt to deal with the rehabilitation process without the assistance of an experienced workers' compensation lawyer. Vocational rehabilitation counselors, in the vast majority of cases, are not on your side. It is their job to terminate your benefits, either by your becoming employed or by taking advantage of your failure to cooperate and thereby have your benefits terminated. It is in your best interests to return to work at suitable employment. You should, therefore, fully cooperate with all reasonable vocational rehabilitation efforts. See Section 22.

7. Failure to Accept Suitable Employment.

It is in your best interest to accept suitable employment whether at your prior job or at a new job that may be presented to you. The law does not (and should not) allow a worker to collect workers' compensation benefits if he can work. On the other hand, you are not required to accept any job that your employer or their vocational rehabilitation worker finds for you. The work must be "suitable" to you based upon your physical limitations, age, education, training, and experience. It is important to work closely with an experienced workers' compensation lawyer to help you determine whether the job offered to you is suitable. See Sections 20 and 21.

8. Failure to Anticipate That You Will Be Followed and Videotaped.

It is a mistake to assume that you will not be followed and be videotaped by private investigators. Insurance companies would rather pay money to private investigators and lawyers than pay you. You should assume that a private investigator will be watching your every move outside of your home. In some cases, they even look inside your home. See Sections Q and R.

9. Working Outside Restrictions When You Return to Work.

If a doctor allows you to return to work, he may restrict some of your activities, such as lifting above a certain weight or raising your arms above your head. If these restrictions are giving, you should follow them explicitly. When you return to work, there is a temptation to follow your supervisor's instructions even if those instructions would have you working in excess of the limitations your doctor imposes upon you. This is a serious mistake. Carry the doctor's written restrictions with you when you return to work and, if your supervisor tries to coerce you into working outside of those restrictions, give a copy of those restrictions to your immediate supervisor and politely tell that supervisor that your doctor will not allow you to work outside those restrictions. See Section 20.

10. Settling Your Claim Without the Benefit of An Experienced Workers' Compensation Lawyer.

It is a serious mistake to assume that your employer and its insurance company will treat you fairly. You should understand that in the vast majority of the cases, they will take advantage of you if you let them. The professionals who work for your employer and the insurance company know workers' compensation law inside out. They are looking after themselves, not you. Always seek the advice of an experienced workers' compensation lawyer before you sign any agreements. See Sections G and 24.

11. Assuming That Rehabilitation Counselors Are Your Friend.

Rehabilitation counselors are working for your employer and the insurance company. They are not working for you. See Section 21.

12. Allowing the Employer to "Doctor Shop."

If your employer accepts your claim and agrees to pay, he does have a right to direct your medical care. However, once your medical providers have been established, he cannot switch you to another doctor without the permission of the Industrial Commission. Insurance companies like to have you seen by doctors who they can count on to "sing their song." Do not allow them to do this. If your employer or its insurance carrier attempts to switch you to another doctor, consult an experienced workers' compensation lawyer immediately. See Section 22.

13. Failure to ask for a Second Opinion.

The law allows an injured worker to obtain a second opinion if the worker is not satisfied with the opinion of the doctor concerning the nature and extent of impairment. You should consider asking for a second opinion. However, it is not always wise to ask for a second opinion. This decision is case specific. You should consult with an experienced workers' compensation lawyer to help you decide whether you should ask for a second opinion. See Section 22.

14. Assuming That the Compensation Rate Set by the Employer is Correct.

Most of the benefits you are entitled to receive from your workers' compensation claim are based upon your average weekly wage. The average weekly wage includes the gross amount of your pay before any deductions. Average weekly wage may also be increased because of certain allowances your employer may provide such as a housing allowance. Do not be shortchanged by settling for an incorrect compensation rate. See Section 13.

15. Failure to Seek Medical Care.

Many injured workers, especially males, try to "shake it off" after they are injured at work and fail to seek appropriate medical attention. It is not unusual for a person to have significant injuries without realizing it. If an injured worker waits several days or weeks before seeking medical attention, the claim is suspect. This delay in treatment gives the employer still another excuse to deny the claim. If you have been in an accident, always get examined by a doctor, even if you do not think you are seriously injured. See Section F.

SECTION E
QUICK ANSWERS TO QUESTIONS YOU MAY HAVE ABOUT YOUR WORKERS' COMPENSATION CLAIM

Question:

Will I be followed by a private detective after I make my workers' compensation claim?

Answer:

If your on-the-job injury is serious enough to require you to be out of work for an extended period of time, you will almost certainly be surveillanced by a private detective who will follow you around, probably in a paneled truck or van trying to take video footage of your activities. Because of the strong likelihood of being followed, you should assume that you are being followed and act accordingly. See Section Q.

Question:

If my doctor assigns work restrictions which limit what I can do at work, such as the amount of weight I can lift and whether I can bend and stoop, should I work outside of those restrictions when I return to work?

Answer:

No. Not only is it detrimental to your health to work outside of the physical restrictions that your doctor has given you, but it will also hurt your case. See Section 20.

Question:

Should I settle my case without the assistance of an experienced workers' compensation lawyer?

Answer:

No. It will be difficult for you to know what your case is worth and whether the insurance company has offered you a fair settlement offer. However, if your case is very minor and does not involve your being out of work for any substantial period of time or any permanent injuries, you do not necessarily need a lawyer. However, you should probably get a consultation from a lawyer before settling a case, even if it is a relatively small case. See Section 24.

Question:

Are the vocational counselors who are assigned by the insurance company interested in my welfare?

Answer:

No. These vocational rehabilitation counselors, both medical and vocational, work for the insurance company. Their involvement in your case is for the benefit of the insurance company, not you. See Section 21.

Question:

Am I entitled to a second opinion by a doctor of my choice regarding the nature and extent of my disability?

Answer:

Yes. See Section 22.

Question:

What is my workers' compensation rate or my "comp rate"?

Answer:

For most people, it is two-thirds of your average weekly wage (this is gross wages, not take-home pay). There are, however, certain minimum and maximum comp rates. See Section 13.

Question:
Can I recover money for my pain and suffering involved with my on-the-job injury?

Answer:
No.

Question:
Am I entitled to a jury trial to decide my workers' compensation case?

Answer:
No.

Question:
Is it necessary for me to be a United States citizen in order to collect workers' compensation benefits?

Answer:
No, you do not have to be a citizen nor do you have to be properly documented in order to collect workers' compensation benefits.

Question:
How long do I have to be employed before I am entitled to workers' compensation benefits?

Answer:
There is no required length of employment. If you are injured at work on the first day of employment, you will be entitled to full workers' compensation benefits.

Question:
If a doctor has treated me for work-related injuries, is it permissible for the doctor to send me a bill?

Answer:
No. It is against the law for a doctor to charge a patient for treatment of a work-related injury. See Section 22.

Question:
If a worker is killed in a work-related accident, what can his family recover?

Answer:
Generally the family will be able to recover two-thirds of the deceased worker's average weekly wage for a 400-week period. If the family members are themselves disabled, they could possibly receive benefits for longer than 400-weeks. See Section 13.

Question:
May I recover if I am injured as the result of horseplay on the part of myself or a co-worker?

Answer:
Yes, in most cases. See Section 14.

Question:
If I am assaulted while at work, may I recover workers' compensation benefits?

Answer:
Yes, you can recover, unless the assault is not work-related. See Section 14.

Question:
May I recover workers' compensation benefits if I am injured in a storm or from other weather-related incidents?

Answer:
Yes, if the injury is clearly work-related. See Section 14.

Question:
If I am injured while traveling to work, can I recover workers' compensation benefits?

Answer:
The answer, in most cases, is no. Workers' compensation law does not protect workers who are injured while traveling to work or while traveling home after work. There are certain exceptions, however. For instance, traveling salesmen who have to drive regularly in their work can recover, even if they are traveling to their first sales appointment of the day. For a discussion on certain other exceptions to the general rule, see Section 14.

Question:
Is it necessary that an accident occur in North Carolina in order to collect workers' compensation benefits?

Answer:
No. For a discussion of the requirements in order to collect for accidents which occur outside of North Carolina, see Section 14.

Question:
If I injure my back at work, without there being an accident, may I still recover workers' compensation benefits?

Answer:
Yes. See Section 14.

Question:
If I become unable to work due to repetitive motions over long periods of time, can I recover workers' compensation benefits even though I was not in an accident?

Answer:
Yes, for a discussion on when you can recover for repetitive motion conditions see Section 14.

Question:
To what benefits am I entitled if I have been injured in a work-related accident?

Answer:
The benefits for injured workers fall under three main categories:

1. Wage replacement, which generally equals two-thirds of the worker's average weekly wage while he is out of work.

2. Payment for all medical expenses related to the on-the-job injury or illness.

3. Compensation for permanent injury to parts of the body. The amount of benefits available for permanent impairment depends upon the particular part of the body affected and the degree of impairment. In addition, a worker may recover for disfigurement caused by scars or other conditions. The family of a deceased worker killed in a work-related accident may recover benefits for at least 400 weeks. See Section 13 for further discussion on benefits available to workers' compensation claimants.

BRENT ADAMS

Question:
Who decides whether a claim will be paid if my employer refuses to pay voluntarily?

Answer:
The North Carolina Industrial Commission. The case is heard initially by a Deputy Industrial Commissioner. Either party has a right to appeal a Deputy Commissioner's decision to the full Industrial Commission. See Section 19.

Question:
How does the law define "disability"?

Answer:
Disability under the workers' compensation law means the incapacity, because of an injury or occupational disease, to earn the wages which the injured employee was receiving at the time of his injury. See Section 16.

Question:
If my work-related accident injures a part of my body which had previously been injured, can I still recover?

Answer:
Yes. For a discussion of pre-existing conditions, see Section 16.

Question:
If my employer is late in paying my weekly workers' compensation benefits, what can I do?

Answer:
If an employer is more than fourteen days late in making a workers' compensation payment, the Industrial Commission will impose a ten percent penalty. This penalty should give enough incentive to the employer to pay benefits on time.

33

Question:

How long will I continue to receive workers' compensation payments?

Answer:

Until you are able to go back to work earning the same (or greater) wages that you earned before your injury. If you can never go back to work, you are entitled to weekly compensation benefits for the rest of your life. See Section 13.

Question:

Is there any way I can recover weekly workers' compensation payments in an amount greater than two-thirds of my average weekly wage?

Answer:

Yes, if your injury was caused by your employer's willful failure to comply with a law or a safety regulation, your employer will have to pay you a ten percent increase in benefits. See Section 17.

Question:

If my work-related injury was my fault, can I still collect?

Answer:

Yes, you can still recover full workers' compensation benefits even if the accident was caused by your own negligence.

Question:

If my on-the-job accident happened because I was under the influence of alcohol or illegal drugs, can I still recover?

Answer:

No. There can be no recovery if the worker is intoxicated or under the influence of controlled substances and if that intoxication or influence of controlled substances caused the injuries. See Section 18.

Question:

What happens if I do not cooperate with the vocational rehabilitation counselor assigned to me?

Answer:

Your workers' compensation benefits will be suspended until you demonstrate that you are willing to comply with all vocational rehabilitation efforts. For a discussion on how to deal with vocational rehabilitation counselors, and how to avoid the suspension of your benefits, see Sections 21 and P.

Question:

If my employer or his workers' compensation insurance carrier tell me to go to a certain doctor to be examined, must I do so?

Answer:

Yes. If you fail to do so, your benefits may be suspended until you demonstrate that you are willing to be examined by a doctor of your employer's choice. See Section 22.

Question:

Who decides what doctors will treat me for my work-related injuries?

Answer:

If your employer accepts responsibility for your accident and pays your claim, the employer gets to dictate your medical care to a certain degree. However, once a treating doctor is established, the employer cannot "doctor shop" by sending you to doctor-after-doctor until he gets the report he wants. In order to change your treating physician, you and your employer must seek permission from the Industrial Commission.

Question:
When I am being treated by a doctor for a workers' compensation injury, must the doctor keep what I tell him secret?

Answer:
No. In a workers' compensation setting, there is no physician-patient privilege. Your doctor can tell your employer or its insurance carrier anything he or she learns from you regarding the workers' compensation case and your injury/illness.

Question:
How long will my employer be required to pay all of my medical expenses incurred in connection with my work-related accident?

Answer:
The law says that the right to payment for medical expenses shall terminate two years after the employer's last payment of medical workers' compensation payments. However, if it is anticipated that medical expenses will be incurred past the two-year deadline, the Industrial Commission will issue a special order requiring payment of these benefits even if they are incurred more than two years from the date of the last medical payment. You must take affirmative action to be sure that your employer will have to pay you for expenses which are incurred after two years. Without this special order, the two-year limit applies.

Question:
What happens if my condition gets worse after my benefits stop?

Answer:
If your condition worsens after an order or supplemental award of benefits is made, you can apply to the Industrial Commission for additional benefits. You must do so, however, within two years from the date the last compensation payment was made. If you have entered into a "clincher" agreement which has been approved by the industrial commission, you can never ask for additional benefits. See Sections 23 and 24.

Question:
What is a "clincher agreement"?

Answer:
An agreement whereby the employer pays a lump sum to the employee in exchange for a release by the employee and an agreement to never make any further claims is commonly referred to by lawyers and insurance adjusters as a "clincher agreement." These agreements must always be approved by the North Carolina Industrial Commission, otherwise they are not valid. Once approved by the Industrial Commission, however, the employee may never again collect any money for that workers' compensation claim. This is true even if the injured worker's condition gets worse. See Section 24.

Question:
Does my employer ever have to pay in advance for my weekly workers' compensation benefits for total disability?

Answer:
No. The employer is only required to pay for total disability benefits on a weekly basis. There are no situations in which

these payments are required to be paid in advance. If, however, a "clincher agreement" is made, the employer will voluntarily make advance payments. Otherwise, the disabled employee must accept benefits on a weekly basis.

SECTION F
THINGS YOU SHOULD DO IMMEDIATELY AFTER YOUR ON-THE-JOB INJURY

When someone is injured in an accident, whether work related or otherwise, the last thing he is thinking about is claims, lawsuits, and receiving money. However, there are a few things an injured worker should do as soon as possible after an accidental on-the-job injury. The failure to take these precautions could make it difficult for you to collect your workers' compensation claim.

The most important thing to do after you've been injured is to seek proper medical care (Refer to Section 22). Seeing a doctor early is a precaution you should take in order to protect your health. An additional benefit of seeing the doctor early is that it will help to establish your workers' compensation claim. If you wait several weeks to see a doctor after you've been injured, the delay raises questions about whether you were actually injured on-the-job. The insurance company will try to claim that you were injured in some other activity outside of work.

When you first see the doctor or other health care professional, be sure to tell him that you were injured while at work. Give him as much detail as possible about how the accident happened, what the accident did to your body, what you experienced at the time of and immediately after the accident and all other details necessary for a doctor to understand what happened and how it affected you physically.

Try to recall and write down the names of all coworkers who may have witnessed your accident. These witnesses could be important if there is any dispute about whether you were in an accident or how the accident occurred.

The law requires that an injured worker give his employer written notice of the accident within 30 days of the occurence. Report the accident in writing and give the written report to the appropriate person at your job. The proper person would be your supervisor or the human resources department or someone else in management. The safest course is to Xerox several copies of your written report and give it to more than one person. Also, it is a good idea to mail the written report to the appropriate address of your employer. Do not panic if you are reading this more than 30 days after your accident. Although the law requires you to make a written notice to your employer within 30 days from the date of the accident, failure to do so will usually not prevent you from collecting. See Section 15.

In an emergency situation, you should seek treatment from the first doctor available. However, once the emergency has subsided, you should give your employer a chance to choose your doctors and other health care providers. If your employer accepts responsibility for your claim, your employer has the right to direct your medical care and to decide what doctors you should see. Outside of an emergency situation, if you choose your own doctor without allowing your employer to be involved in the decision, it may be difficult to require your employer to pay for that doctor.

From the first opportunity immediately after the accident and throughout the entire claims process, you should keep a written diary of all important information relative to your accident and your claim. You should make a written account

WORKERS' COMPENSATION IN NORTH CAROLINA

to yourself of how the accident happened, your trips to the doctor, your conversations with your employer's management and with representatives from the insurance company.

SECTION G
DO YOU NEED AN ATTORNEY TO HANDLE YOUR WORKERS' COMPENSATION CASE?

In a perfect world, a workers' compensation claimant should never need a lawyer.

North Carolina law protects injured workers and provides a reasonable set of benefits for the injured worker. The North Carolina Industrial Commission, which administers the workers' compensation law, provides a mechanism for injured workers to enforce the payment of benefits which the law allows.

In a perfect world, all employers and their insurance companies could obey the law and willfully provide for the employee all the benefits to which he is entitled.

However, we do not live in a perfect world. Employers and their insurance companies are profit-making entities. Employers are usually corporations, most often big corporations, who have no soul and no conscience. Insurance companies are always corporations and likewise have no soul and no conscience. Their goal is to save themselves as much money as possible by shortchanging the injured employee.

That being said, however, it is a fact that the vast majority of workers' compensation claims are not contested and no lawyer is ever involved.

It could very well be that you will not need a lawyer to help you with your workers' compensation case.

If your employer and its insurance company treat you fairly and provide for you all the benefits to which you're entitled, you do not need a lawyer. This book is a very helpful guide for you to determine the benefits to which you are entitled. By reading the relevant sections of this book, you will have a general idea as to what your employer and its workers' compensation carrier are obligated to do for you.

If you have a question as to whether your employer is treating you fairly, you may want to call the ombudsman division of the North Carolina Industrial Commission. The number to call for an ombudsman is 1-800-688-8349. This ombudsman will counsel you, answer your questions, and help you determine if you're getting all you are entitled under the law.

If the ombudsman is not able to completely satisfy your inquiry, and if your questions are not answered in this book, you should consult with a lawyer.

Most cases involving minor injuries and limited time out of work will not justify the expense of a lawyer. However, if there are serious injuries which maybe permanent or which involve long periods of time out of work, you should at least contact a lawyer for a consultation.

Most lawyers will not charge for an initial consultation and your issues may be solved without hiring a lawyer.

There are certain critical stages, however, in which a lawyer should be involved in order to prevent costly mistakes which may be easily avoided with proper legal advice. Among these stages are the following:

1. When your doctor tells you that you have reached "maximum medical improvement." See Section 13.

2. When your employer notifies you that work is available for you but you do not feel that you are physically able to return to work. See Section 20.

3. When you sense that you are being followed and videotaped by private detectives. See Section Q.

4. When your employer files a motion with the Industrial Commission to terminate your workers' compensation benefits. See Section 20.

5. When the insurance company tells you that they want to settle your claim on a "clincher agreement." See Section 24.

6. When your family member has been killed and in a work-related accident and you are making a claim for workers' compensation benefits. See Section 13.

7. When a vocational rehabilitation counselor has been assigned to your case. See Sections 21 and P.

8. When the nurse rehabilitation counselor is talking to your doctor outside of your presence or when they insist on being in the examination room with you and the doctor when you are being examined. See Sections N and 21.

9. Any time that you just "don't feel right" about your employer and any of its representatives and you do not feel that they are treating you fairly.

When you consult with a lawyer, there is no requirement or obligation that you actually hire that lawyer. In many cases, a short conference with a lawyer will be all you need to solve your problem. Most lawyers will not charge for an initial consultation. If the lawyer feels he cannot help you, he will tell you so, usually without any cost or obligation.

See Sections I and J for guidelines on how to find the right workers' compensation lawyer.

SECTION H
HOW DO YOU LOCATE A GOOD WORKERS' COMPENSATION LAWYER?

Choosing a workers' compensation lawyer should be done with great care. It is an important, but difficult, task. Your selection of a lawyer should not be based upon advertising alone. Look at the yellow page ads in your community. You will see that the ads are all basically the same. One does not have to be a good lawyer to buy a big yellow page ad or to have commercials on television. You should not even hire *me* unless I can convince you that you can trust me to do a good job for you.

SECTION I
HOW DO YOU CHOOSE THE RIGHT WORKERS' COMPENSATION LAWYER?

There are certain questions that you should ask that will lead you to the best lawyer for your case, no matter what type of claim you have. This will involve some time on your part, but that should not matter because the decision of which attorney to hire is very important.

The law is becoming more and more complex every day. It is virtually impossible for a lawyer to be fully competent in all areas of the law. The field of workers' compensation law is especially complex. In our opinion, these cases should not be handled by a lawyer who does not concentrate his or her practice in the field of workers' compensation law. Too many cases have been lost by lawyer mistakes made by lawyers who try to spread themselves too thin and practice in many different areas of the law. Too many cases are settled too cheaply and are virtually "given away" by lawyers who handle a lot of workers' compensation cases, but who will not or cannot go to hearing when the insurance company does not offer an adequate settlement. Insurance companies are very much aware of which workers' compensation lawyers will take them to the Industrial Commission and who will not. One of the first things insurance companies want to know when they evaluate the case is who is representing the injured party. **If this information is important to the insurance company, it should certainly be important to *you* when deciding which lawyer to hire.**

If you hire a lawyer who has never tried a substantial case or who runs a settlement mill and settles all of his cases, you may not be well served. I believe it is so important that you hire the right lawyer to handle your case that I will send you the name and telephone numbers of lawyers in my area who I know to be good attorneys that you should call if you do not become my client. Just call me at (910) 892-8177 or e-mail me at *brent@brentadams.com* and I will send you the list.

Why would I give you the names of my competition? The reason is that we are all on the same side in fighting the insurance industry. These lawyers are people for whom I have a great deal of respect. It is my desire that all victims of work-related injuries have their cases handled properly by the right lawyers and that they not end up in the hands of a part-time workers' compensation lawyer or a settlement mill where the case may be "given away" for far less than it is worth.

We offer the following suggestions for finding a good workers' compensation lawyer in your area. They are as follows:

- Get a referral from a lawyer you know. He or she will probably know a specialist in the area of law that you are interested in.

- The yellow pages may be a good source of names. However, you should understand that not everyone advertises in the yellow pages. Most of our cases come from referrals from our satisfied clients or from people who have heard about us in the community. When examining the yellow page ads, look for ads that claim an expertise in too many areas of law. No one can do everything well. You should always be careful of the full-page yellow page ads, especially the double-page ads. These ads tend to generate a lot of cases for the law firms who pay for these ads. Be sure the law firm you choose does not have too many cases to handle effectively and that your case does not get buried under a pile of other cases. You deserve to have your case given top priority and for it to be handled as expeditiously as possible.

- The North Carolina Bar Association has a lawyer referral service, which we recommend. Understand, however, that lawyers on this list of referrals have paid a fee to be listed in this service. Their names come up on a rotating basis. It is, however, a good source for an initial appointment. Use the questions that we give you in this book for the interview.

- Interview several attorneys in your area. Ask each one who else handles your type of case. If an attorney will not give you an answer to this question, that could be a warning signal. The names that keep being referred to by these

WORKERS' COMPENSATION IN NORTH CAROLINA

various attorneys are probably a good indication of which attorneys in your area handle your kind of case on a regular basis. This may be the best way to find a lawyer who is right for you. Ask each lawyer if he has information like we have provided in this book or if he has a web site with similar information so that you can find out more about their qualifications, experience and the way he will handle your case.

• Be cautious if a lawyer tries to pressure you into signing a contingency fee contract. A lawyer should be willing to represent you on an hourly fee basis if you choose. You should take the written contingency fee contract home, read it, understand it and discuss it with your family.

• If you are contacted by a "runner" who hangs out in hospital emergency rooms, police stations or other places where tragedies occur, run the other way. The practice of making uninvited in-person solicitations by lawyers or agents of lawyers, including "runners," is strictly prohibited. This type of conduct will get an attorney disbarred, and rightly so. Even though this conduct is illegal and strictly prohibited, we keep hearing rumors that this practice does exist. If you are approached by one of these uninvited "runners," please call the North Caroline State Bar at 919-828-4620 and report that conduct and then give the name and number of the lawyer that the runner recommends.

• Be cautious if a lawyer tries to direct you to certain doctors for your treatment. The decision of which doctor should treat you for your injuries is yours to make. It could severely hurt your case if it is revealed that you went to a certain doctor because your lawyer told you to. One of the functions of a good workers' compensation lawyer is to know the qualifications of the best doctors who practice in his or her area in certain specialized fields of medicine such as orthopedics, neurology, rheumatology, etc. It is sometimes helpful to your case for you to be examined by one of these specialists for the purpose of assessing your injuries. However, any time a lawyer refers you to a doctor, it could be a very delicate situation, which, if handled inappropriately, could backfire and damage your case.

SECTION J
NINE QUALIFICATIONS YOUR LAWYER SHOULD HAVE

The following are suggestions about areas of inquiry you should make with a prospective lawyer. It is not necessary for a lawyer to meet all the criteria suggested below; however, if many of these criteria are absent, you should be concerned as to whether this lawyer is suitable to handle your case.

Experience. Experience is a big factor in most cases. It only makes sense that the longer a lawyer has been practicing in a particular area of law, the more skilled you would expect that lawyer to be. However, experience alone certainly does not make for a good lawyer. It is necessary for a lawyer to continue to learn, grow and develop in his or her area of practice. The mere fact that a lawyer has been practicing for a long time does not in and of itself mean that he or she is sufficiently qualified to handle your case. A lawyer should grow and develop and not handle cases the same way each time, but rather to continually improve his or her techniques and methods. Insurance companies tend to give greater credence and respect to lawyers who have actually tried cases in court. The greater number of cases actually tried and substantial verdicts and settlements achieved, the more likely it is that insurance companies will listen to the lawyer. Of course, the past successful experience of the lawyer is no guarantee of future results. However, a long track record of successfully trying cases is a good indication of that lawyer's level of experience and success.

Trial Experience. Ask the lawyer how many cases he actually tried. Have they achieved any significant verdicts or settlements? Does he have a list of verdicts and settlements available that you can look at? As mentioned elsewhere in this book, insurance companies tend to value cases based in part on the reputation of the lawyer and the number of cases the lawyer has actually taken to trial.

Appellate Court Experience. It is sometimes necessary to appeal a workers' compensation case to an appellate court. In North Carolina, we have two appellate courts: The Court of Appeals of North Carolina and the Supreme Court of North Carolina. Appeals are necessary when the North Carolina Industrial Commission makes an error at law. You would be surprised at how often such mistakes occur. The rate of reversals in the appellate courts is higher than you would suspect. Therefore, a good trial lawyer needs also to be a good appellate lawyer. If not, you may need to hire a separate lawyer to handle an appeal. Ask your prospective lawyer how many cases he has actually appealed to our appellate courts.

Respect in the legal community. Does your prospective lawyer teach other lawyers courses on trial practice in continuing legal education programs sponsored by bar associations, trial lawyer organizations, and law schools?

Board certification. The National Board of Trial Advocacy tests and certifies trial lawyers. It requires a minimum number of trials and recommendations from judges and opposing attorneys. You should ask your lawyer if he or she is board certified. You can also go to the web site for the

◆

National Board of Trial Advocacy and see which lawyers in
your area are board certified.
http://www.nbtanet.org/directory/index.php

Membership in the Million Dollar Advocates Forum.
Membership is limited to lawyers who have won million and
multi-million dollar verdicts and settlements. Less than 1%
of U.S. lawyers are members. In order to be a member of the
Million Dollar Advocates Forum, a lawyer must have
demonstrated exceptional skill, experience, and excellence
in advocacy by personally achieving a trial verdict, award, or
settlement in the amount of one million dollars or more. Each
case is different, however. Just because your lawyer is a
member of the Million Dollar Advocates Forum does not
mean that your case will be tried or settled for anywhere near
one million dollars.

Leadership positions in trial lawyer organizations. See if
your prospective lawyer is a member of the North Carolina
Academy of Trial Lawyers. Ask him if he has ever held any
legal leadership positions in that organization. The North
Carolina Academy of Trial Lawyers is an active group of trial
lawyers who work hard to improve the trial skills of their
members and who provide specialized courses in trial
practice for their membership. Ask if the lawyer has spoken
at any of these trial practice seminars. The American
Association for Justice (formerly the Association of Trial
Lawyers of America) is a national organization dedicated to
the training of trial lawyers who only represent accident
victims. Members of the Association for Justice do not
represent big corporations or insurance companies; they only
represent individuals who have been damaged by the
wrongful conduct of others. Ask the prospective lawyer if he
is active in that organization, if he has ever held positions of

leadership in that group, or if he has ever given lectures and seminars conducted by the American Association for Justice.

Manuscript publication? Has the prospective attorney written any manuscripts on the subject of trial practice for use in teaching lawyers and helping them improve their trial skills? Such publications are another sign of the respect that the legal community has for this lawyer's skill and experience.

Available and information? Ask the prospective lawyer how he intend to keep you informed about the progress of your case. In our practice, we send our clients a copy of every piece of correspondence and pleadings in the case, both incoming and outgoing. We also keep the client fully informed on the progress of their case and we keep then advised of the various steps of the proceedings and when they can anticipate the next activity to take place. Clients are invited to call or email us at any time. If we cannot personally return your call right away, one of my assistants will help you set up a specific telephone appointment. We also encourage our clients to make an appointment for an in-person consultation at any time that it is convenient for them. Any law firm you are considering should provide you with this level of communication.

SECTION K
TV TRIAL LAWYERS WHO NEVER WERE

One of the law firms which advertises heavily on television in the Raleigh/Durham/Fayetteville, North Carolina area uses Robert Vaughn, a TV and movie personality probably most famous for his role in "The Man From U.N.C.L.E.", in its television advertisements. These ads usually end with the phrase "we mean business."

This law firm sued the North Carolina State Bar because it would not allow the firm to televise an ad which contained a fictional dramatization which created the impression that insurance companies, that would otherwise contemplate bad faith tactics, would decide to settle a personal injury claim at the mere mention of the attorney's name.

The United States District Court upheld the North Carolina State Bar's prohibition of the use of this ad and found that it was inherently misleading. In so holding, the court noted that there was evidence presented by the head of the law firm itself that the head of the law firm:

"HAD NEVER TRIED A CASE, WITH THE EXCEPTION OF SITTING AS SECOND CHAIR IN ONE TRIAL IN WHICH THE OPPOSING PARTY PREVAILED."

In addition, the court noted that there was evidence that no attorney in that law firm had ever tried a case under the trade name of that law firm. Farrin v. Thigpen, 173 Fed. Sup. 2d, 427. This case may be read online at ncpersonalinjurylaw.com.

North Carolina is not the only state in which citizens have been exposed to misleading lawyer advertising. The Supreme Court of Arizona found that a law firm's advertisements implying that it was willing and able to try, and actually did try, personal injury cases was misleading where no attorney at the firm had ever tried a personal injury case to a conclusion. In the Matter of Zang, 154 Arizona 134, 741 P.2d 267, 275 (1987)

SECTION L
ATTORNEY FEES

Most lawyers will represent workers' compensation claimants on a contingency fee basis. Under that arrangement, if there is no recovery to the claimant, the lawyer will not charge a fee. However, if there is a recovery, the lawyer agrees to accept a certain percentage as the total fee.

Most lawyers charge a contingency fee of 25% of the total recovery at the initial hearing. Some lawyers increase the percentage if there are appeals to the full Industrial Commission or to the North Carolina Court of Appeals.

All fees, including attorney's fees, must be approved by the North Carolina Industrial Commission. It is against the law for a lawyer to collect a fee in a workers' compensation case before that fee has been approved by the North Carolina Industrial Commission.

In certain limited situations, it may be possible to have the Industrial Commission require the employer to pay all or a portion of the claimant's attorneys fee.

If the employer and its insurance company appeal an initial determination of a case by a deputy insurance commissioner, the Industrial Commission may, but is not required to, order the employer and its insurance carrier to pay reasonable attorney's fees necessitated by the appeal. If the case is appealed from the full Industrial Commission to the Appellate courts, the employer and its insurance carrier may be required to pay reasonable attorney's fees to the employee.

If the Industrial Commission finds that any hearing has been defended without reasonable grounds, it may require the defendant and its insurance carrier to pay the employee's attorney's fees. Under the statute which allows such fees, attorney's fees may be awarded even at the initial hearing. It is unusual for the Industrial Commission to require an employer to pay attorney's fees under this provision of the law.

The Industrial Commission usually finds that there is some reasonable grounds for defending a claim even in those cases in which there is practically no merit or reasonable justification to deny the claim.

The employee should not count on recovering attorneys fees from the employer. However, it does happen and the employee should always try to recover attorney's fees from the employer and its insurance carrier.

SECTION M
HOW TO HANDLE JOB INTERVIEWS

It is important to cooperate fully with all vocational rehabilitation efforts. It is important that your conduct at a job interview not be interpreted as an attempt to sabotage your chances of returning to gainful employment.

You should arrive early for the interview. You should be appropriately dressed and present a positive upbeat demeanor to the person conducting the interview.

You should have an accurate and complete resumé. This resumé should fairly and accurately set out your job skills, but it should not be exaggerated. Certainly, there should never be any misstatements in your job interview.

You should not volunteer that you have suffered an injury of any kind. This voluntary statement on your part may be

WORKERS' COMPENSATION IN NORTH CAROLINA

interpreted as an attempt to sabotage your chances of getting hired. Of course, if you are asked about any prior injuries, you must answer truthfully both verbally and on any documentation to which you are furnished.

At this interview, you should learn the prospective employer's skill requirements as well as the physical demands of the job for which you are applying. It would make no sense for you to apply for a job for which you obviously are not qualified. For instance, if you cannot type and have had no experience in using a computer, it would be foolish to apply for a job which requires computer skills.

Be sure to get the interviewer's signature on your job search log **(see Appendix)** to prove that you actually went for the interview.

SECTION N
HOW TO DEAL WITH THE DOCTORS

Medical evidence is usually the key to winning or losing workers' compensation disability benefits. It is therefore important to have a good relationship with the treating doctors, even those chosen by the insurance company.

The most common mistake the injured employee makes upon his first visit to the doctor is not adequately reporting the facts of the accident to the doctor.

It is difficult to prove that the visit to the doctor is related to an on-the-job accident when the doctor's notes do not contain any reference to the on-the-job accident. You would be surprised at how often this occurs. It is therefore important to report the facts to the doctor and report them frequently.

You should understand that everything you tell the doctor could very well be read by the North Carolina Industrial Commission, the body which will find the facts in case of a dispute. Therefore, it is important not to make any intemperate or unwise statements to the doctor.

Many times the doctor does not himself make entries into the medical records. It is important to determine who actually makes the notes and be sure that they are done accurately. It is surprising how frequently inaccurate facts are recorded in doctors' records. Unfortunately, once these inaccurate facts are in the record, it is almost impossible to have them removed. If the doctor does not testify until a year-and-a-half after the injury, the doctor will likely have no independent recollection of the visit. It is very unlikely that a doctor would admit that any entry in his record is wrong.

It is important to get copies of the medical records frequently and to correct any errors that exist in the records as nearly as possible to the date they were entered. The longer you wait, the more difficult it is to correct the mistake.

You should, of course, be truthful with the doctor so that he or she can treat your injury as effectively as possible.

If possible, try to get the doctor to agree to discuss with you his opinion about return to work restrictions, functional capacity results, or anything relating to your ability to return to work before he gives the information to the insurance company in writing or otherwise. Many times a nurse rehabilitation professional will try to unfairly influence the doctor's opinions with respect to these issues. You should at least have an opportunity to present your views to the doctor on an equal basis with the nurse. With respect to an honest doctor, there is no reason why your input should not be just as influential to the doctor as that of the nurse hired by the insurance company. The vast majority of doctors are honest and have your best interests at heart. With respect to the very few dishonest doctors, there is little you can do, but it does not hurt to try.

Be sure to specifically request that you be present for any and all conferences between the doctor and any rehabilitation counselor, nurse or vocational counselor. Although the rules specifically prohibit a rehabilitation professional from communicating with the doctor outside your presence, the doctor himself may request such a private meeting. If so, such a private meeting would probably not violate the rules. It is therefore important that you express to the doctor your desire to be present at all meetings with the nurse or vocational counselor. Doctors are generally very careful to observe patient/physician privileges. While the privilege does not technically exist with respect to workers' compensation matters, a doctor will very likely be sensitive to your request to be present for these interviews and the request should always be made.

Be sure not to express any negative feelings or attitudes about the rehabilitation counselor or the workers' compensation insurance company to your physician. It will reflect badly upon you. Chances are the doctor is well aware of workers' compensation nurse rehabilitation counselors and how they operate. You will not be telling him anything he does not already know.

No matter what, do not lose your temper with the doctor. He or she is the one whose opinion is a huge factor in whether you win or lose your case. Even if you end up with one of the few medical prostitutes, do not show your anger.

Some lawyers advocate tape recording all visits to the doctor's office. This is a very ticklish issue. I would advise against recording any of visits with the treating doctor. It will more than likely antagonize the doctor and ultimately do more harm than good.

With respect to a one-time doctor's examination by one of the non-treating medical providers, I would advise the injured worker to take a tape recorder with him during the examination and to keep this tape recorder in the record mode during the entire time the worker is in the presence of the doctor. This will show how cursory the examination will likely be and will avoid any disputes at a later time as to what was said to the doctor. However, even with respect to the adverse examining doctor, common sense should be used and the doctor should not be provoked or agitated unless absolutely necessary. At the very least, keep accurate notes about the doctor's adverse examination, especially concerning the time the doctor was actually with you in the examining room, what he or she actually did to examine you, and how much time was spent examining you.

When being examined or treated by your workers' compensation doctor for on-the-job injuries, be sure that the doctor does not treat you for any unrelated conditions at that same visit. If the workers' compensation carrier notices that the record shows that the doctor treated you for anything unrelated to your workers' compensation injury, he may disallow payment for the visit and require you to pay the entire bill yourself. If you need to see this doctor for something unrelated, be sure to keep the visits separate and distinct from your workers' compensation treatment.

If the doctor prescribed over-the-counter medication, request that he give you a prescription for a similar medication that requires a doctor's prescription. Otherwise, the workers' compensation carrier may not pay for the nonprescription medication.

SECTION O
SIX RULES FOR DEALING WITH MEDICAL REHABILITATION PROFESSIONALS

What steps should an employee take to protect his rights in the face of involvement of medical rehabilitation professionals? We suggest the following:

1. Never allow a medical rehabilitation professional to have a private conference with a doctor.

The rules specifically provide that the worker be offered the opportunity to attend any conferences between the rehabilitation professional and the physician. The worker has an absolute right to be present for all conferences between the doctor and the rehabilitation professional. The only exception to this rule is if the physician holds the opinion that it is "medically contraindicated for the worker to participate in the conference." If this unlikely event should happen, the rehabilitation professional must note that fact in his or her report, and he must include in that report the substance of the communication. There are other very limited exceptions relating to scheduling meetings, requests for medical records, and other very limited situations. However, when such communications are made outside the presence of the injured worker, and without his or her consent, the rehabilitation professional must document the reasons for and the substance of the private communications.

2. *Always insist upon a private examination by the doctor outside the presence of the rehabilitation professional.*

The rules give the injured worker the absolute right to this private examination, and the rehabilitation professional cannot be present unless the worker consents.

3. *Never let the rehabilitation professional switch the treating physician without your consent.*

One of the areas of greatest abuse of the system by workers' compensation insurance companies is their habit of "doctor shopping" when the authorized treating physician renders opinions which the insurance company does not like. These opinions usually fall into the category of work restrictions and the capacity of the employee to return to work.

Unfortunately, there are a few doctors who are little more than medical prostitutes. These are the doctors to whom insurance companies always send claimants for examination or treatment when they want an opinion that the worker is able to return to work without restrictions or with very few restrictions.

The lawyers who handle workers' compensation cases on a regular basis know who these doctors are and know what they are going to say even before the worker is seen by the doctor. The insurance industry knows that these doctors will "sing their song" for the money they are paid and will make every effort, legal or illegal, to be sure that the injured worker is seen by that doctor. These very few doctors are paid hundreds of thousands of dollars each year by insurance companies to do their "dirty deeds." These doctors are a disgrace to their profession, as well as to the administration of workers' compensation claims.

As long as the employer accepts the responsibility for paying a workers' compensation claim, the employer is entitled to direct the medical care of the employee. The employer is entitled to initially choose the physicians who will treat the claimant. These physicians thereby become the workers' "approved" treating physicians. Once treating physicians for the employer are established, the employer is not allowed to switch the treating physicians without the approval of the N.C. Industrial Commission.

Even though the employer is not allowed to "switch" treating physicians, it is the widespread practice for insurance companies to "doctor shop" when they do not like the opinions of the initial approved treating physician. The employers and their insurance companies can only get away with this if they are allowed to by the employee. Unless an employee is represented by an experienced workers' compensation lawyer, the insurance company will direct the employee to go from doctor to doctor until one of these doctors renders an opinion which the insurance company likes.

It is usually the rehabilitation nurses who direct this doctor shopping practice. They all know the few medical prostitutes who will sing their song.

The choice of the physician is extremely important. In most cases, the doctor's testimony literally means the difference between winning and losing. That is why you should be extremely careful not to let the insurance companies switch doctors. The insurance company does have a right to have you examined by a physician of their choice even though that physician may not be the authorized treating physician. There is not much you can do about the choice of that physician. However, you can fight the attempt by the insurance company to switch treating physicians. A treating physician, particularly if he or she has been a treating physician for an extended period of time, is in a much better position to form opinions concerning the nature and extent of the injured employee's disability, Therefore the opinion of that doctor usually carries greater weight with the Industrial Commission than does the opinion of an examining physician who only has seen the patient one time.

4. Be careful not to make careless statements to the medical rehabilitation counselor.

The medical rehabilitation counselor may encourage the employee to make statements indicating that his condition is better than it really is. If you talk to the nurse on a good day and relate that you are feeling much better and feel that your condition is markedly improved and fail to report on the many days that you're having bad days, that one-sided report may give a false impression to the treating doctor. Many times the treating doctor bases his opinion on what is reported to him or her by the rehabilitation nurse.

5. Ask the rehabilitation nurse for copies of all reports.

It is important to check these reports for accuracy to be sure your symptoms are correctly reported to the doctor, and that the nurse is correctly reporting what the doctor has told you about your condition.

Workers' compensation insurance case managers rely heavily on reports from the medical rehabilitation nurses. It is unfair to the injured worker for rehabilitation nurses to skew their reports to show that the injuries are not as severe as they truly are.

6. Keep your lawyer informed.

Keep your lawyer informed of any significant discussions with your nurse rehabilitation counselor. The performance of the nurse rehabilitation counselor is important. It is therefore essential that you keep your lawyer informed if you feel that the nurse rehabilitation counselor has taken a position contrary to your interest or is working against you in obvious ways. Any concerns that you have with your rehabilitation counselor should be discussed with your attorney.

SECTION P
SEVENTEEN RULES TO BEST DEAL WITH VOCATIONAL REHABILITATION PROFESSIONALS

1. Always have your lawyer present during your first meeting with the rehabilitation counselor.

The Industrial Commissions regulations, which apply to vocational rehabilitation counselors, provide that, if requested, the first meeting of the worker with the rehabilitation professional shall take place in the office of the worker's attorney. This meeting is extremely important and should always be requested. At this meeting the injured worker's lawyer will let the vocational rehabilitation professional know that the lawyer is familiar with the rules applicable to vocational rehabilitation counselors and will insist that those rules be followed. These rules, some of which will be discussed below, are an important protection for the injured worker. One of the chief weapons that vocational rehabilitation counselors use to wear down the worker and harass the worker to the extent that he becomes willing to settle the claim too cheaply is to create a lot of busy work for the injured employee. The vocational rehabilitation counselor will, for instance, send the worker in search of jobs that the counselor knows the worker is not qualified to perform. This first meeting with the lawyer helps discourage this activity by the vocational rehabilitation worker and makes the life of the injured employee easier.

2. Don't make careless statements to the rehabilitation counselor.

Often times an injured worker will make statements to a vocational rehabilitation counselor to the effect that: "I am not going to look for any job that doesn't pay at least $15.00 per hour", or "I can't work any job so I am not going to even apply." Vocational rehabilitation counselors love to hear this kind of language from the injured worker. They report these statements to the insurance company and make it appear as if the worker is refusing to cooperate with vocational rehabilitation efforts. If the Industrial Commission believes that the worker, in fact, is refusing to cooperate with vocational rehabilitation efforts, the worker's benefits will stop. The law allows the Industrial Commission to "suspend" benefits only so long as the refusal to co-operate with rehabilitation procedures continues. As a practical matter it is most difficult to get workers' compensation benefits reinstated once they have been suspended for failure to comply with efforts to rehabilitate the worker. The worker should convey to the rehabilitation counselor that he appreciates the rehabilitation effort by the counselor and he is willing to cooperate fully and completely with any and all reasonable efforts at rehabilitation.

3. Return to work as soon as possible.

At our law firm, we always encourage the injured worker to return to work as quickly as possible.

The worker earns more income and has a more positive image of himself when he is working. Work is good. It is good for the financial and mental health of the entire family that the worker is employed earning a good income. Most injured workers had much rather be at work earning an income than staying at home and becoming a burden to their family.

This does not mean, however, that you should jeopardize your health or go back to work before your doctor says that you are ready.

4. Don't make overly optimistic statements to the rehabilitation counselor.

Rehabilitation counselors strive to coax a worker into saying that he is capable of doing just about anything, even when the worker knows he can't. The counselors will take these statements, blow them out of proportion, and use them against the worker in a termination hearing. They will ask the workers such things as whether he can climb a ladder, if he can use hand tools, if he does his own dishes or mows the lawn. If the worker says, "No, I can't climb a ladder or use hand tools," the counselor may ask, "Are you sure? I think you probably could. Would you be willing to try?" There is a great temptation to respond: "Yes, I will try; I think I may be able to." Again such statements will be blown out of proportion and used against the worker. The injured worker should always tell the vocational counselor, and everyone else, the absolute truth. However, he should not be unfairly led into making statements that overstate his true physical capacity.

5. Get a copy of the rules.

The rules require that the vocational rehabilitation counselor provide the injured worker a copy of the rules for rehabilitation professionals. Be sure to ask for these rules and read them. It is important for injured workers to know the rules so they will be aware when the vocational counselor steps out of line (and the worker will step out of line in almost every case). If the vocational counselor fails to give you the rules, report that fact to your attorney who will supply you a copy of the rules.

6. Don't let the vocational rehabilitation counselor talk you into going into business.

Most people have an idea in the back of their minds that some day they would like to go into business for themselves. This is not the proper time for such an endeavor by an injured worker. The vast majority of small businesses fail within the first year or two. It is unrealistic to count on income from a small business. We once had a vocational counselor who argued that our client was no longer disabled because he could go into the tattoo parlor business. This worker had never been in business for himself and had no experience in operating a business. He just had a general vague notion that he would like to be in the tattoo parlor business. The Industrial Commission would never use such a business plan to terminate the benefits of the worker. However, many times workers are lulled into settling their case for less than it is worth by a vocational rehabilitation counselor who convinces the worker that he could succeed in business with the money he received from settling his workers' compensation claim. This is very dangerous.

7. Beware of "make work" jobs.

Insurance companies sometimes convince employers to offer the injured worker a position which bears absolutely no resemblance to a real job that they would hire someone else to perform. Such a job is considered "make work." That is, it is not a real job, but it is a job created simply for the purpose of giving this worker something to do. The illusion is that, if the worker goes back to work at this "make work" position, he is no longer disabled. An example would be a disabled yard and maintenance worker who is illiterate and is given a "job" of sitting in a room and reviewing manuals, catalogues and equipment maintenance books. Even if this unfortunate worker could read, that would not be a job that the employer would pay someone else to do. Such a make work job may be appealing to the worker since it does not involve heavy lifting, or outside work, and he will receive a pay check. However, what the worker does not understand is that once workers' compensation is out of the picture and he is no longer considered disabled, this job will certainly disappear along with the worker's paycheck. It is always important, however, to consult with your attorney before you turn down any job.

8. Stay in close contact with your attorney.

The point in a workers' compensation case at which a vocational rehabilitation counselor gets involved is the most dangerous time in the claims process. It is during this time that facts can occur which may form a basis for the termination of benefits. Keep in close contact with your lawyer and tell him or her every detail of what is happening between you and the vocational rehabilitation counselor. Consult with your attorney each time a job is offered to you, each time a new rehabilitation program or course is offered to you, and at each time anything occurs with the rehabilitation counselor that causes you to feel uneasy. If you win your claim, your lawyer will be paid. Make him or her go to work for you. Call us often. That is what we get paid for, to advise you at each stage of this complicated process.

9. Do not let them into your house.

There is no reason for the rehabilitation counselor to come to your home. You should never meet him in your home but instead meet him in a neutral place such as a library or restaurant. As mentioned above, the first conference should be in the lawyer's office with your lawyer present.

The danger of having any meetings in your home with the vocational rehabilitation counselor is that it gives the counselor unfair access to your private life and information about you and your family which could be turned against you. Along these same lines, your personal life is no business of the rehabilitation counselor and you should not share your information about your personal life with him. The less your workers' compensation carrier knows about your personal life, the better off you are.

10. Insist on a vocational assessment and plan.

The Industrial Commission rules require that before job placement activities may be started, the vocational rehabilitation counselor must complete a vocational assessment and must prepare a formulation of an individualized plan for vocational services which specifies its goals and the priority for return-to-work options in each case. This assessment and individualized plan could be of great value to the injured employee and may help him or her return to the job market. While all vocational rehabilitation counselors are required to prepare these documents, it is very rarely done; at least, it is rare for it to be done properly. Notice that the rules provide for an "individualized plan." That is, the plan must be specifically tailored for the individual injured worker. This is almost never done. You should insist that the vocational counselor do his job by providing you with these very important documents.

11. Insist on "suitable employment"

The rules require that before an injured worker may be sent out to apply for a job and sit for an interview for that job the vocational rehabilitation counselor, by use of the vocational assessment and by the formulation of an individual plan for vocational services, must determine that the job is suitable for the employee.

Over the years of our practice it has been the norm and not the exception for vocational counselors to attempt to send our clients to interviews for jobs that were obviously unsuitable for them. For instance, a roofer who was unable to read and write was sent to apply for jobs requiring computer skills. Or, a worker with a 10-pound lifting restriction was sent to interview for a job in which he would be required to lift 30 pounds on a regular basis. Many times the vocational rehabilitation counselor would instruct the worker to go to the want ads and to apply for every job in the want ads. Other times, the vocational rehabilitation counselor would get a list of potential jobs from the Employment Security Commission and ask the employee to spend his time, money and effort to travel around a radius of 20 or 30 miles seeking jobs without any prior determination as to whether those jobs were suitable for the worker.

The rules define "suitable employment" to mean: "Employment in the local labor market or self-employment which is reasonably obtainable and which offers an opportunity to restore the worker as soon as possible and as nearly as practicable to pre-injury wage, while giving due consideration to the workers' qualifications (age, education, work experience, physical and mental capacities), impairment, vocational interest and aptitudes." There are several important phrases in the above definition. For instance, *"local labor market"* means that jobs which require driving a long distance away from the workers' home would not be suitable. *"As nearly as practicable to pre-injury wage"* means that a highly-paid construction worker should not be required to apply for minimum-wage-paying jobs.

12. Insist on vocational training.

The rules require that the vocational rehabilitation counselor consider formal vocational training to prepare the worker for a job with the current or new employer as a return-to-work option. Insurance companies almost always oppose such vocational training. Insist on this training if you feel that it will help you get back into the work force.

13. Always go to interviews.

Always go to job interviews. This rule may seem inconsistent with the statements made above. However, the old adage "two wrongs don't make a right" has great application here. Even though vocational rehabilitation counselors frequently violate the rules of the North Carolina Industrial Commission, you should be absolutely pristine in your conduct. Therefore, you must go to all interviews even if there has been no vocational assessment or individualized plan. This is true even though the job for which you are asked to apply is clearly not suitable for you.

There are several reasons for this caution. The primary one is that you do not want to give the insurance company any reason to terminate your benefits. If you fail to attend a scheduled job interview the insurance company could ask the Industrial Commission to terminate your benefits because you are not cooperating with their efforts to rehabilitate you. While you may think that you should not be required to

attend a particular job interview, you can never predict how
the Industrial Commission would rule. Why put yourself in
that position? This is a battle you do not need to fight. Let
your lawyer fight that battle for you.

Another reason is that if there is ever a hearing, you want to
show the Industrial Commission that you have done
absolutely everything possible to rehabilitation yourself and
to get back to work.

The way to insist on proper performance by the vocational
rehabilitation counselor is to have your lawyer petition the
Industrial Commissioner to have that counselor removed.

Even though it is a hassle to go to useless and unproductive
job interviews, by doing so you are helping to ensure that you
will continue to get workers' compensation benefits. Your
weekly workers' compensation benefits are fairly good pay
for doing all that is required by even the most abusive
vocational rehabilitation professional.

14. Fully know and understand your job description.

Have a good idea of the job description for the job on which
you were injured. The vocational rehabilitation professional
may at some point show to the doctor a written or videotaped
job description. The doctor will be asked to render an opinion
as to whether you can do that job based upon the job
description submitted by the vocational counselor. Rules
require that this job description must be submitted to the
injured employee prior to its submission to the doctor. It is
important to examine that job description to be sure if it is
accurate. If the job description submitted by the vocational
counselor is not accurate, you must make objections or
amendments to this job description. This is a job for your

lawyer and he or she will take care of that responsibility for you. However, it is important for you to have a good understanding of your job description and discuss this with your lawyer. Your lawyer has not worked in your job and will have to rely upon you in large part to help determine the accuracy of the job description submitted by the vocational rehabilitation counselor.

15. *When going for a job interview have the person who interviews you sign a statement indicating that you were present for the interview.*

It adds credibility to your testimony concerning your job search efforts to have signed acknowledgments to help prove that you actually went for job interviews. Ask the person who interviews you to sign a short statement which acknowledges that you came for the interview. It will help to have a pre-typed form for the potential employer to sign on the spot. Do not rely upon their promise to send something later. Get that signature before you leave. See the job search log in the appendix.

16. *Keep accurate notes about each job interview and about each conference with the vocational rehabilitation counselor.*

After each job interview conference or interview with the vocational rehabilitation counselor, write down as closely as you can remember everything that was said. These notes may be very useful later on. See the job search log in the appendix.

17. *Get rid of that rascal.*

The Industrial Commission rules provide that a rehabilitation professional may be removed from a case upon motion by either party for good cause shown. Good cause would be the failure of the rehabilitation counselor to follow the rules applicable to rehabilitation professionals. An example of the most flagrant violation of the rules is a vocational rehabilitation worker continuously sending a worker for interviews for jobs that he or she is obviously not suited to perform. The rules provide in three separate places that a vocational counselor should not initiate or continue placement activities which do not appear likely to result in the placement of the injured worker in suitable employment. Report these violations to your attorney and ask your attorney to remove this rehabilitation counselor. Even if the motion to remove is denied, the fact you attempted to remove him may help enforce the rules. From that point on the vocational rehabilitation counselor may think twice before he continues to flagrantly violate the rules.

SECTION Q
BE CAREFUL OF THE SNOOPS

If you are out of work because of a workers' compensation injury, it is most likely that at some time before your claim will be concluded you will be under surveillance or followed around by private detectives hired by the insurance company. Of course, it is their purpose to videotape you doing physical activity in order to show that you are not disabled and that you are faking your claim.

You should just assume that they are following you every minute because if they are not doing it now, they will surely do so in the future.

There are many things that you are likely to do outside of your house that could be incorrectly construed as evidence that your physical abilities are greater than those stated by your doctor.

These private detectives are professionals and are extremely skilled in gathering evidence to use against you.

Workers' compensation claimants are usually angry when they learn that they are being followed by a private detective. However, this anger should not be directed to the private detectives. They are simply doing the job they were hired to do. It is important to remember that these private detectives have no animosity towards you; they are simply doing their job.

Any anger you display towards these private detectives will almost certainly come back to haunt you. An example of this is the worker, who upon realizing he was being followed and videotaped, turned around and "mooned" the private detective. Of course, nothing could have pleased the insurance company more. The doctor's report stated that this worker could not bend over. Obviously when the worker bent over to moon the detective, the insurance company then had proof that the worker indeed could bend over. In addition, this worker was charged and convicted of indecent exposure.

The best way to deal with the private detective is to pretend that you do not know he is there. The injured worker should do nothing outside the confines of his home that could be construed as evidence that the worker has physical capacity beyond that being claimed. This means that you should never mow your lawn, rake your yard, take out the trash, wash your car or do anything that even remotely could be construed as physical labor. Be careful when going shopping. Do not carry grocery bags outside. Have somebody do all these tasks for you.

SECTION R
THE DIRTY TRICKS

While the work that private detectives do to gather evidence for insurance companies is honorable work, some do cross over the boundaries of honesty and fair dealing. Some examples of the dirty tricks these private detectives engage in are the following:

1. Placing a few dollar bills on the steps leading out of an injured workers' house or beside his car in an effort to try and catch the injured worker bending over to pick up the dollars.

2. Staging a bogus free gift of some heavy object like a case of motor oil or soft drinks. When the injured worker arrives to pick up his "prize," the private detective is there to film the worker bending down to pick up the motor oil or soft drinks.

3. Letting the air out of an injured workers' tires in the hope that the worker can be filmed changing a tire.

4. Paying a neighbor of the injured worker to videotape views of the worker through a window and offer the neighbor an extra bonus if he is able to catch the injured worker doing activities which may be construed as vigorous or strenuous.

5. Many times workers try to mow their grass and find they can only operate their lawnmower short periods of time. The private detective could videotape the worker for many hours and have only a few minutes of footage showing the worker mowing grass over a period of several days. If this is done during the spring or fall when the worker may wear

the same coat every day, the detective may splice the film together take out all the footage which shows no activity and splice the combined footage showing all the lawn mowing in order to make it appear that the lawn mowing was one continuous activity without any breaks.

The suggestions made in this section are not intended to encourage the injured worker to defraud or mislead the insurance company. On the contrary, we always urge our clients to be upfront and honest and straight forward in all of their dealings. However, evidence gathered by private detectives can be very misleading. If a worker is seen carrying grocery bag into the house, the videotape does not know whether the grocery bag is filled with paper towels or heavy firewood or soft drinks. The suggestions contained in this section are intended to avoid any misleading impressions that can be made from the work of private detectives. Detectives can set up surveillance of an injured worker for weeks or months and end up with very little footage. Out of this footage of perhaps five or six hours, the detective will show only that part, perhaps ten minutes of footage showing physical activity on the part of the worker. We advise our clients to avoid being the victim of this type of activity, not in order to mislead or defraud the insurance company, but to prevent false impressions from being created.

Although some detectives do step out of bounds, the work they perform does serve a useful purpose. Of course, there is a rare minority of people who do fake their injuries and exaggerate their claims. These people are guilty of insurance fraud and should be prosecuted and put in jail for their misconduct. It is the activity of this rare minority of cheaters which makes it difficult for the vast majority of truly injured workers to receive fair treatment from their employer and its workers' compensation carrier. We applaud and commend these detectives for this work. It should be understood that those who would seek to defraud an insurance company constitute an extremely small percentage of workers' compensation claimants. When insurance cheaters are caught, it makes for sensational news. For every three minutes of videotape footage showing a cheat who claims to be disabled playing basketball, there are years of videotape footage showing honest injured workers doing ordinary mundane tasks well within the restrictions placed upon them by their physicians. The insurance companies do not give this footage to John Stossel. The rare incidence of insurance fraud creates a distorted picture for the public which is unfair to the honest injured worker.

SECTION S
YOU CAN WIN THIS WAR

Insurance companies have declared war on injured people. The moment you were injured, you became "public enemy number one" to the insurance company. They will malign you and attack your character. They will pry into your personal and medical history to try to find embarrassing facts to use against you. They will use anything in your past, whether or not it has anything to do with your claim, to harass you, beat you down, and discourage you from seeking the money you deserve. They began fighting you even before you became injured. For years insurance industry publicity and advertising campaigns have tried to create in the minds of the general public an image of the injured person as someone who is unworthy of credibility and respect. The insurance industry wants the public to hate the injured people and to think of them as liars and cheaters as someone who are seeking something for nothing. The purpose of this unfair smear campaign is to try to convince jurors, even before you are injured, that you should not recover for the personal injury inflicted upon you by a negligent driver.

Their purpose is also to persuade law makers (U.S. Congressmen and State Legislators) to do away with long standing laws which protect all citizens from harm from drunk drivers and other wrongdoers. The insurance industry calls this "tort reform."

The success that insurance companies have had in tainting the minds of jurors has caused them to offer "law ball" settlements and has forced injured people to either accept their inadequate offers or go to court.

However, when you have a meritorious claim and have suffered personal injury, insurance companies will pay an adequate award if they know you will go to court to protect your rights.

That is where we come in. We will show the insurance company that we will take them to court with your meritorious claim.

If you have a valid claim, this is a war that can be won against the insurance company. We will help you "make things right."

PART II

Injured Workers' Guide To North Carolina's
Workers' Compensation Law

SECTION 1
INTRODUCTION

Compared to many states, North Carolina has a very good workers' compensation law. However, the benefits to be received from our workers' compensation law are far less than could be expected from a similar injury sustained in an automobile collision or other incident arising from the negligence of another person arising outside the work place. This is because North Carolina's workers' compensation law limits the amount which can be recovered for injury or illness caused in the work environment. There are certain things that victims do not get in workers' compensation claims. Chief among these is payment for pain and suffering. Pain and suffering is not an element of damage which can be collected in workers' compensation cases.

SECTION 2
THE PURPOSE OF THE WORKERS' COMPENSATION LAW

The purpose of the Workers' Compensation Act is to provide for the injured worker or his dependents in the event of his injury or death, at the cost of the industry which he was serving.

The North Carolina Supreme Court has written that the primary purpose of the Workers' Compensation Act is to compel industry to take care of its own wreckage and to provide compensation benefits for industrial injuries. The Supreme Court has also written that the purpose of the Workers' Compensation Act is not only to provide a swift and certain remedy to an injured worker, but also to ensure a limited and determinate liability for employers.

The general purpose of the Workers' Compensation Act is to substitute for common law or statutory rights of action and grounds for liability, a system of monetary payments by way of financial relief for loss of capacity to earn wages.

One purpose of the Workers' Compensation Act is to relieve against hardship, rather than to afford a full compensation for injury. The section of maximum and minimum awards in industry is a compromise. It is not the purpose of the Workers' Compensation Act to relieve or absolve employers from the consequences of their negligent conduct.

The Workers' Compensation Act was enacted to provide swift and sure compensation to injured workers without the necessity of protracted litigation.

The Workers' Compensation Act is a compromise arrived at through the concessions of employees and employers alike. Nothing in it supports the notion that it was enacted just for the protection of careful, prudent employees, or that employees that do not stick strictly to their business are beyond its protection. By its terms, with certain exceptions, the Act applies to all employees who work for employers with the requisite number of employees and are injured by accident during the course of and arising from their employment; and it is not required that the employment be the sole proximate cause of the injury, it being enough that any reasonable relationship to the employment exists, or employment is a contributory cause.

The philosophy which supports the Workers' Compensation Act is that the wear and tear of human beings in modern industry should be charged to the industry, just as the wear and tear of machinery has always been charged.

The Workers' Compensation Act is primarily for the protection and benefit of the employee.

Workers' Compensation laws are a statutory compromise, which assures workers' compensation for injuries arising out of and in the course of employment, without their having to prove negligence on the part of the employer. In exchange for the employer's loss of common law defenses, however, the employee gives up his right to common law verdicts. In effect, the common law tort liability law was replaced with no-fault liability in the work environment.

However, the Workers' Compensation law is not the equivalent of general accident or health insurance. In order to obtain a recovery under the Workers' Compensation Act the worker must show that his injury sprang from the employment.

The Workers' Compensation Act is to be liberally construed to effectuate the broad intent of the Act to provide compensation for employees sustaining an injury arising out of and in the course and scope of employment, and no technical or strained construction should be given to defeat this purpose. The courts favor a liberal construction of the Workers' Compensation Act in favor of the claimant.

SECTION 3
WE NEED TO PROTECT NORTH CAROLINA'S WORKERS' COMPENSATION LAW

It is bad news if you have been injured in a work-related accident. However, if you have to be injured in a work-related accident, it is good that your case will be governed by North Carolina workers' compensation law. North Carolina has one

WORKERS' COMPENSATION IN NORTH CAROLINA

of the better workers' compensation laws compared to those laws in some other states.

North Carolina's workers' compensation laws certainly do not provide a "windfall" to injured workers. It was never intended that they should. However, it is intended that the workers' compensation law give injured workers and their families some level of security and salary continuation when they are injured in a work-related accident. North Carolina law does a very good job of achieving that goal. You will read about the specific provisions of the law in other sections of this book. Generally, the wage replacement for injured workers in North Carolina is two-thirds of the workers' average weekly wage. Because workers' compensation benefits are generally not subject to state or federal income taxes, this two-thirds wage continuation is fairly close to what most workers would realize after taxes from their regular salaries.

The workers' compensation statutes in North Carolina are generally very fair to the worker. North Carolina's appellate courts which have interpreted workers' compensation laws also have been fair to the worker.

It is required in law that the workers' compensation laws be construed liberally in favor of the worker. North Carolina appellate courts have generally honored that rule.

Your medical providers should also be glad that they practice in North Carolina. All fees for services rendered by doctors, hospitals and other healthcare providers must be approved by the North Carolina Industrial Commission. The same rule applies in most other states. However, the North Carolina Industrial Commission has been awarding fees to medical providers in an amount greater than that realized by medical providers in most other states. While the doctors do not usually get their full fees approved, compared with other states, the fees approved are reasonable.

While injured workers do benefit from good workers' compensation laws in North Carolina, we cannot take those laws for granted. The political body which enacts statutory law in North Carolina is the North Carolina General Assembly. Each time the General Assembly meets, there is a new and vigorous attack upon our workers' compensation law. This attack is mounted by big business, big manufacturers, the United States Chamber of Commerce, and, of course, big insurance companies. These special interest groups spend hundreds of millions of dollars a year across the country attacking and seeking to change the workers' compensation laws in all states so as to deprive this nation's working public of benefits when they are injured in service of their employers. This concerted effort has been successful in many states when the representatives of the people cave in to the big money interest groups and sacrifice the rights of their constituents.

There is a grave risk that this can and will happen in North Carolina. North Carolina's General Assembly has, for the most part, stood up fairly well against the assault of the "tort reformers" who pay big money to lobbyists and others in an effort to have legislation passed that takes away the rights of North Carolina citizens who are the victim of on-the-job injuries or negligent drivers, negligent doctors, and the manufacturers of defective products.

One glaring example of how North Carolina state senators and members of the House of Representatives sold out to the special interest groups occurred in 1996 when the General Assembly enacted draconian legislation which put a ceiling on the amount that North Carolina juries could set as punitive damages for wrongful conduct. This latest legislation, which was passed by state legislators who consider themselves "conservative," threw out established law which had been serving the people of North Carolina well for over 300 years. This law gutted the rights of North Carolina citizens and made it less costly for big manufacturers, big banks, big insurance companies, negligent doctors, and other special interest groups to engage in conduct which should be punished and therefore which give rise to punitive damages. It is inconceivable to me that members of our General Assembly, elected by the people of North Carolina, would consciously and on purpose vote for legislation which is against the interests of their constituents but which enriches out-of-state big money interests. In my own little county there are no big manufacturers, no insurance companies, no big banks and no big special interest groups. Our little county is made up of honest, hard-working people who have to work for a living to make ends meet. Yet, their state senator at the time voted against their interests and instead voted for the interests of the out-of-state big money wrongdoers. He voted for the limitation on punitive damages and against the people in his county. Why would he do that? For one thing, the good people of my county were busy making a living and were not paying attention. Had they known what was being done to them and given a chance to vote, they would surely have voted against it. So this state senator could vote for this legislation without much opposition from his constituency. Money does not just talk; it screams bloody murder.

It is ironic that these "tort reformers" who seek to throw out longstanding, well-established rules consider themselves to be "state's righters" who generally oppose any legislation giving power to the federal government and vote to keep the power, as closely as possible, in the hands of local government. Yet these same "tort reformers" think it is

BRENT ADAMS

perfectly fine to let the Congress in Washington or the
General Assembly in Raleigh tell Harnett County juries or
Franklin County juries that they do not have the power to
enter a verdict in their discretion and that they must limit their
verdicts to a certain amount set by Congress or the North
Carolina General Assembly. This legislation, which caps the
amount a jury can set, in effect, allows the politicians in
Raleigh to tell Harnett County jurors and Franklin County
jurors what to do.

Pardon the personal political statement set out above.
However, I relate that true example of raw political power
only to point out that North Carolina's workers'
compensation laws are in great danger. We should be vigilant
to elect legislators who will serve the interests of the people
and who will not turn their backs on the people in favor of the
big money special interest groups.

SECTION 4
THE NORTH CAROLINA INDUSTRIAL
COMMISSION

North Carolina workers' compensation law is administered
by an administrative agency known as the North Carolina
Industrial Commission.

As stated above, it is bad if you are injured while working;
but it is good that your case will be dealt with in North
Carolina. The North Carolina Industrial Commission is one
of the reasons why you are fortunate that your case will be
decided in North Carolina.

The North Carolina Industrial Commission is a body
consisting of seven commissioners who devote their full time
to the duties of the Commission. The commissioners serve

for a period of six years. The law provides that not more than three appointees shall be persons who can be classified as representatives of employers and not more than three appointees who can be classified as representatives of employees.

The North Carolina Industrial Commission does a good job of administering workers' compensation laws in a manner that is fair to both the employer and the employee. Members of the Commission work hard and take their jobs seriously.

The Industrial Commission serves as judges and juries and decides all issues of fact when there are factual disputes.

The North Carolina Industrial Commission has a huge workload and efficiently handles that workload even in spite of financial restraints imposed by North Carolina's tight budget.

The Industrial Commission is on the cutting edge of technology and has created a web site which is recognized all across the country as the best workers' compensation web site. The URL is *www.comp.state.nc.us* and the site contains extremely valuable resources and tools for anyone who is interested in workers' compensation law.

The former chairman of the North Carolina Industrial Commission is Mr. Buck Lattimore, an extremely skilled administrator and jurist. Under his leadership, the North Carolina Industrial Commission was careful to give all claimants and employers a good fair hearing without partiality to either side and, at the same time, efficiently dispose of cases so that there was no undue delay in rendering decisions. This is very important, especially from the standpoint of injured employees who need to have their cases heard quickly.

Recently, Pamela Young, a commissioner of the Industrial Commission was appointed chairperson. Chairperson Young has distinguished herself as an astute lawyer and a skilled and impartial jurist. It is expected that she will lead the Industrial Commission in the fine tradition of former Chairman Lattimore.

North Carolina taxpayers are served well by the North Carolina Industrial Commission.

SECTION 5
WORKERS' COMPENSATION ACT IS THE ONLY AND EXCLUSIVE REMEDY

As part of the compromise between business and labor, the workers' compensation law provides that the injured employee may not sue his employer in court nor is the injured worker entitled to a trial by jury.

In a court of law, the injured party is entitled to a full recovery for his injuries. This recovery would include an amount for pain and suffering and all other elements of actual damage suffered by an innocent victim. The injured worker does not have this right.

In a workers' compensation claim, which can only be made to the North Carolina Industrial Commission, benefits are strictly limited to the elements of damage discussed in this book.

There is a very narrow exception to that rule, which only arises when the employer requires the employee to do work that is so dangerous that it is substantially certain in advance to cause the employee serious injury or death. However, the application of this exception is very rare.

This same rule prohibits all suits against co-employees for conduct resulting in an on-the-job injury. The exclusive remedy is through the workers' compensation law.

The trade off for the injured worker is that he or she is not required to show that someone else was at fault in causing the injury. Negligence does not have to be established. The worker can recover full workers' compensation benefits even if he alone is at fault in causing the injury.

SECTION 6
CLAIMS AGAINST THIRD PARTIES

We have discussed within section 5 that an injured worker may not bring a lawsuit in court against his employer or a co-employee for injuries or occupational diseases which arise out of and in the course and scope of employment. The injured workers' only remedy for workers' compensation injuries is through the North Carolina Industrial Commission. If a worker is injured as a result of the negligence of someone who is not employed by the same employer as the worker, the injured worker may sue that negligent party. Lawyers refer to this as a "third party claim."

The "third party" is any person who is not employed by the same employer as the injured worker.

The injured worker could therefore have two separate and distinct claims arising out of the same accident. The most common example of two claims arising out of the same accident involves the use of motor vehicles.

One example arises when a delivery person for UPS is injured by the negligence of a third party while driving the delivery truck. In that case, the delivery person would have a claim against his employer because he was injured by accident arising out of and in the course and scope of his employment. The delivery person also has a claim against the negligent driver for negligence in operating a motor vehicle which caused the delivery person injury. This claim against the negligent driver can be brought in state court. The claim can be tried by jury and the injured worker can recover his full damages, including pain and suffering from the negligent driver.

It is at this point that the injured UPS delivery person should consult with an experienced workers' compensation lawyer to determine how to proceed on both of these claims.

If the injuries are serious enough that the UPS delivery person is out of work for an extended period of time, a workers' compensation claim should be filed. The advantage of the workers' compensation claim is that it is usually paid quickly so that weekly workers' compensation payments can assist the injured worker and his family while he is out of work. In addition, the employer will pay all medical expenses. This relieves the worker from paying any deductible or co-pay on his health insurance. The disadvantage is that the amount of recovery is limited.

The advantage of the third party claim for negligence brought in state court is that the worker can collect full damages including recovery for pain and suffering. The disadvantage is that it usually takes much longer, especially in the case of a significant injury.

In most cases it is advantageous to make both claims simultaneously. By doing so the worker will usually receive workers' compensation payments quickly while pursuing the third party claim.

In accidents involving less severe injuries wherein the injured worker does not miss work, the better course is usually to forego the workers' compensation claim and proceed only with the third party claim. This is especially true if the worker has health and hospitalization insurance to cover medical bills.

Most health and hospital insurance policies have a provision which excludes payment for medical treatment incurred as a result of a workers' compensation claim. However, if no workers' compensation claim is made, it is usually not a problem to collect small medical bills from the health insurance carrier.

The employer has a right to collect out of any proceeds from a third party claim the amount which the employer paid as workers' compensation benefits to the injured worker. This is known in law as a right of subrogation. The employer's right of subrogation is a large factor in determining whether it makes sense to bring a workers' compensation claim for minor injuries. Any money that is paid on a workers' compensation claim will be deducted from the third party recovery and paid to employer or its workers' compensation carrier.

With respect to larger injuries, however, the employer's right to subrogation should not weigh against the decision to file both claims simultaneously.

The state court judge has the discretion to eliminate or reduce the workers' compensation subrogation lien. A trial judge would be more likely to reduce or eliminate the subrogation lien if the employee's injuries are severe and if the injured worker is unable to recover from the third party an amount to fully compensate for the injuries.

An experienced workers' compensation lawyer should be consulted to assist the injured worker in making decisions involving third party claims.

SECTION 7
CAN AN INJURED WORKER COLLECT BOTH WORKERS' COMPENSATION AND UNEMPLOYMENT BENEFITS?

In order to make a claim for unemployment benefits, the applicant must state to the Employment Security Commission that he is ready, willing and able to work if he can find a job. If a workers' compensation claimant makes this assertion, it is of course inconsistent with the claim for total disability benefits under the workers' compensation law. If an injured worker can work, he is not entitled to workers' compensation benefits for total disability. If an injured worker cannot do any work, he or she is not entitled to unemployment benefits. These claims are therefore somewhat inconsistent.

However, with respect to an injured worker who is capable of some work but unable to return to his former employment, it is conceivable that the worker could make a valid claim for both unemployment benefits and workers' compensation benefits. A worker who can do some work is entitled to unemployment benefits provided he is actively looking for work. In addition, that same worker is entitled to workers' compensation benefits for his partial disability when he can do some light duty work, for instance, but he is unable to return to his former employment.

North Carolina law prevents a worker from collecting both unemployment benefits and workers' compensation benefits during the same time period. Workers' compensation benefits will be reduced by the amount of unemployment benefits collected by the worker.

Workers' compensation benefits made in payment for impairment of body parts or bodily function are not subject to reduction because of the receipt of unemployment benefits. A tactic frequently used by insurance company defense lawyers to attack the credibility of an injured worker is to ask whether the worker has applied for unemployment benefits. The lawyer knows that if there was such an application the worker would have had to certify that he is ready, willing and able to work. This statement is, of course, inconsistent with a claim for total disability either temporary or permanent. By exposing this inconsistency on the part of the injured employee, the defense lawyer will have achieved his goal of impeaching the credibility of the injured worker.

SECTION 8
WHO IS COVERED BY THE WORKERS' COMPENSATION LAW?

To be covered under the workers' compensation law, a person has to be an employee who is working for an employer. While this may seem obvious, North Carolina's workers' compensation law has some quirks which, unfortunately, leave some employees out and deprives them of the benefit of the workers' compensation law.

In order for the workers' compensation law to apply, the injured workers' employer must regularly employ three or more employees in the business.

The workers' compensation law does not apply to domestic services. Agricultural workers are not covered unless the employer has 10 or more full-time, non-seasonal agricultural workers regularly employed. There are special rules that govern when sawmill employees are covered.

Railroad workers are not covered by North Carolina's workers' compensation law. Instead, they are covered under the Federal Employer's Liability Act (FELA). Employees of state-owned railroad companies are covered. There are also certain exceptions for prisoners, volunteer fireman, and rescue workers.

Sole proprieties and partners engaged in business are not covered unless they buy workers' compensation insurance for themselves.

Casual workers are not covered. Employment is considered "casual" when it is irregular, unpredictable, sporadic, and brief in nature.

SECTION 9
IF YOU ARE INJURED WHILE WORKING FOR A SUB-CONTRACTOR YOU MAY RECOVER FROM THE GENERAL CONTRACTOR

The law provides that anyone who sublets any contract for the performance of any work shall obtain from such subcontractor a certificate proving that the subcontractor has workers' compensation insurance. If this certificate is not obtained, the company or individual who hires that subcontractor will be liable to any injured employees of the subcontractor. This is true even if the subcontractor or general contractor has fewer than three employees working for him at the time of the injury.

WORKERS' COMPENSATION IN NORTH CAROLINA

This is a good law. It protects workers who are employed by financially unsound subcontractors who may employ only one or two workers. This law provides that even though the injured worker's direct employer may have fewer than three employees and may not have any workers' compensation insurance, the contractor for whom that sub-contractor is working is liable to the injured employee. This is true even though there is no direct employee-employer relationship between injured worker and the general contractor.

SECTION 10
IT IS NOT NECESSARY TO BE A UNITED STATES CITIZEN OR TO HAVE PROPER DOCUMENTATION IN ORDER TO RECOVER FULL WORKERS' COMPENSATION BENEFITS

There is no requirement that an injured worker be a United States citizen in order to recover workers' compensation benefits. Neither is there any requirement that the worker have proper documentation. A worker may be an illegal immigrant and still recover full workers' compensation benefits.

You should not hesitate to bring a workers' compensation claim even if you do not have proper documentation to be in the United States.

SECTION 11
NO SPECIFIC TERM OR LENGTH OF EMPLOYMENT IS REQUIRED

There is no required term of employment necessary in order to be entitled to workers' compensation benefits. A person would be entitled to full workers' compensation benefits even if they are injured during the first five minutes of employment.

SECTION 12
INDEPENDENT CONTRACTORS

The workers' compensation law does not apply to an independent contractor. Employers sometimes seek to avoid their responsibility to their employees for workers' compensation benefits by calling them independent contractors.

An independent contractor is one who exercises independent employment and contracts to do a piece of work according to his own judgment and method, without being subject to the person who hires him except as to the results of his or her work.

The test is whether the party for whom the work is being done has the right to control the worker with respect to the manner or method of doing the work, as distinguished from the right merely to require certain definite results conforming to the contract. If the employer has the right to control, it is immaterial whether he actually exercises it.

The issue of whether a worker is an employee or an independent contractor is one which is greatly abused by employers. It is very common for an employer to seek to have all of his employees determined to be an independent contactor so as to avoid the employer's liability under the workers' compensation law. Employers use various methods to falsely seek to impose independent contractor status upon their employees. One method is to stamp a statement on the back of each check made to the worker in which the worker, upon endorsing the check, acknowledges that he is indeed an independent contractor.

Another reason employers like having employees classified as independent contractors is that it helps them (the employer) avoid liability to the state and federal government for withholding and Social Security taxes. Employers do not deduct these taxes from people they claim to be independent contractors but instead send a Form 1099 to the taxing authorities.

The issue of whether a person is an independent contractor is very case specific and sometimes it is not possible to predict in advance how the Industrial Commissions will rule on this issue. That is why it is important for the injured employee, at the outset, to employ an experienced workers' compensation attorney.

EXAMPLES OF CASES HOLDING THAT A CLAIMANT WAS AN INDEPENDENT CONTRACTOR AND NOT AN EMPLOYEE

A person engaged in selling newspapers was held not to be an employee of the newspaper and was therefore held to be an independent contractor when he had authority to solicit subscriptions and was free to select his own methods of effecting sales. This is true, although some degree of supervision was exercised by the newspaper.

A hauler of lumber was considered to be an independent contractor where he hauled logs for the defendant at a specified rate per 1,000 board feet, employed his own helpers, and worked in his own way without any directions from the defendant.

A scallop shucker was held to be an independent contractor when she received no training or instruction as to how to shuck scallops. She used her own equipment and she was paid per pound of scallops shucked; she was under minimum supervision and set her own work hours.

EXAMPLES OF CASES HOLDING THAT A CLAIMANT WAS AN EMPLOYEE AND THEREFORE ENTITLED TO FULL WORKERS' COMPENSATION BENEFITS

An operator of a service station was held to be an employee when he operated his service station for the defendant on a commission basis, being required to keep the business open at certain hours, being told to whom to give credit, and being under the control of the president of the defendant company.

A delivery man for an ice company was considered to be an employee when the defendant furnished a horse and wagon and all necessary equipment. The defendent knew the delivery man obtained a load of ice for which he was charged. It was sold at the defendant's regular retail price and the worker was credited with the amount unsold at the end of the day.

A painter was held to be an employee when the evidence showed that the defendant directed the plaintiff's work, hired his helpers and purchased his supplies.

The lesson from these examples is simply that the injured employee should not accept the employer's contention that he or she is an independent contractor. Just because an employer says that the injured worker is an independent contractor does not mean that the employee is not entitled to full workers' compensation benefits. Independent contractors are not covered by the workers' compensation law and therefore receive no benefits. It is therefore important for the injured worker to be classified as an employee.

If an employer claims that the injured worker is an independent contractor, the worker should retain an experienced workers' compensation attorney immediately. These issues are too complex to be handled by the worker without a lawyer. The issue is too important for the worker to give up on, and the claim should be pursued even though there is a contention that the worker is an independent contractor.

SECTION 13
BENEFITS AVAILABLE TO THE INJURED WORKER

Recovery under North Carolina's workers' compensation laws falls into the following categories: (1) Wage replacement (2) Payment of all related medical expenses; (3) Compensation for permanent impairment to a part of the body; (4) Payment for disfigurement; and (5) Death benefits; (6) Travel expenses; (7) Lodging and meals; (8) Modification to the home; (9) Attorney's fees.

1. WAGE REPLACEMENT

The wage replacement is a payment to the worker while he or she is out of work because of disability. The amount of payment is equal to two-thirds of the workers' average weekly wage. There are certain exceptions. For instance, prison guards employed by the State are entitled to 100% wage replacement if they are disabled as a result of an on-the-job injury. If the worker is out of work for less than seven calendar days, there is no wage replacement benefit. Wage replacement only begins after the seventh calendar day that the worker is out of work because of the on-the-job injury. After a worker is out of work for 21 days or longer, the employer has to pay the employee for the first seven days. If the worker is not out of work for a full three weeks, the employee never has to pay for the first week that the worker is unable to work.

THE ALL IMPORTANT AVERAGE WEEKLY WAGE

Most of the workers' compensation benefits, other than medical benefits, are based upon the injured workers' average weekly wage. It is therefore extremely important for the injured employee to be sure that the average weekly wage is computed in such a manner as to result in the highest possible wage. North Carolina law defines "average weekly wages" as: "the earnings of the injured employee in the employment in which he was working at the time of the injury during the period of 52 weeks immediately preceding the date of injury… divided by 52."

GROSS EARNINGS, NOT NET EARNINGS, ARE USED TO DETERMINE AVERAGE WEEKLY WAGE

Earnings are compiled based upon the gross earnings of the employee before deduction for income tax, withholding, social security taxes, and other mandatory deductions.

The law also provides that: "Wherever allowances of any character made to an employee in lieu of wages are specified part of the wage contract, they shall be deemed part of his earnings." An example of this would occur when housing is provided to the worker.

If, during the relevant 52-week period, the worker was out of work more than seven consecutive calendar days one or more times, these days are excluded from the calculation of the average weekly wage. In such case, the earnings for the remainder of such 52 weeks shall be divided by the number of weeks remaining after the lost time has been deducted. For instance, if during the relevant 52-week period there were two occasions in which the worker missed more than seven consecutive days of work for a total of 21 days missed, the wages earned during that 52-week period would be divided by 49 weeks (52 less the 3 weeks the worker was not working).

In cases in which the injured worker has worked less than a year for the employer before the accident or illness, computing the average weekly wage is more difficult. The law sets out three ways to determine the average weekly wage in those situations. The three methods set out below are listed in the order in which they should be applied until a determination is made that the method chosen is "fair and just to both parties." The statutory definition of average weekly wage sets forth a clear order preference as to the calculation of average weekly wage; and when the first method of calculation can be used, it must be used.

Method No. 1: Divide the employee's total earnings during the time he has worked by the number of weeks worked.

In cases in which by reason of the shortness of time during which the employee has been working for the employer, or by reason of the casual nature of the employment, it is impracticable to use Method No. 1, then the following method should be used:

Method No. 2: The average weekly wage should be determined by comparison to the earnings during the 52 weeks prior to the injury of "a person of the same grade and character employed in the same class of employment in the same locality or community."

Method No. 2 would apply, for instance, in a case in which a highly skilled finish carpenter begins working on a "trial basis" at a much lower wage than he will receive after he demonstrates to his employer that he indeed has the skills of a finish carpenter, where it is contemplated that once a worker proves his skills, his salary will increase commensurate with that of a skilled finish carpenter.

Method No. 3: The statute provides that in the unusual case in which "for exceptional reasons," the first two methods fail to provide a fair result, "such other methods of computing average weekly wages may be resorted to as will most nearly approximate the amount which the injured employee would be earning were it not for the injury." An example of the application of the third method would arise when a worker is paid on a per job basis, and for whatever reason was paid an unusually low rate for his work and only worked 13 weeks during the year. In that case, the Court of Appeals has approved a method of computing the average weekly wage which was based upon the average net income for the two prior years, rather than the income actually earned working for the most recent employer. Such a method, however, would have to be found by the Industrial Commission to be "fair and just to both parties."

Our appellate courts have held that the "fair and just to both parties" determination must result in a determination of average weekly wage in such amount as will most nearly approximate the amount which the injured employee would be earning were it not for the injury, in the employment in which he was working at the time of his injury.

In order to apply Method 3 above to determine average weekly wage, the Industrial Commission must find that the use of the first and second method would produce results unfair and unjust to either the employee or the employer.

When an employee who holds two separate jobs is injured in one of them, his compensation is based only upon his average weekly wage earned in the employment producing the injury.

In a case involving a recently promoted salesman where the promotion resulted in a significant increase in pay, and when this increase in pay was rewarded less than three months prior to the injury, when there was testimony by the employee's superior that the employee would have had further increases, it was held that the findings were sufficient to constitute "exceptional reasons to justify a compensation of average weekly wage by using the wage which was fixed at the amount the employee was earning weekly at the time of the injury." The court reasoned that the wages he was receiving at the time of his injury were not temporary and uncertain, but constituted a fair basis upon which to compute the award.

Another case held that when the injured worked received two raises during the relevant 52-week period, his average weekly wage should be determined by averaging wages actually received during the 52-week period, and then divided by 52.

The two cases mentioned above, which have different results, demonstrate that in these unusual situations in which wages vary during the 52-week period, the Industrial Commission has virtually unbridled discretion to determine the appropriate average weekly wage. Sometimes it is not possible to anticipate in advance how the Industrial Commission will rule.

OTHER AVERAGE WEEKLY WAGE ISSUES

Other difficult average weekly wage issues can arise when the injured employee is paid on a per job basis and incurs his own business and equipment expenses. In such cases, sources of evidence may be the employee's tax return and expense records or evidence of what the employee would have had to pay someone else to do the work for him.

In an unusual and interesting case, the appellate court upheld the Industrial Commission's finding that a football player, who was injured in a pre-season game before being officially accepted as a player on the active roster, earned an average weekly wage of $1,653.85 based on a contract amount of $85,000, and $1,000 signing bonus divided by 52 weeks.

When a trainee was injured, the appellate court held that the Industrial Commission was justified in calculating his wage using his actual wages as a trainee, and was not required to use higher wages that a comparable employee would have made after the training period.

Cash wages are not the only factor to be determined in arriving at the average weekly wage. Employee benefits paid in lieu of wages must also be added to the cash wages paid. The North Carolina Supreme Court has upheld a finding of the Industrial Commission that the value of lodging furnished by the employer to the employee was $100 per week, and that the plaintiff received that lodging in lieu of additional wages. Accordingly, the value of that lodging was added to the cash wages paid to determine the employee's average weekly wage.

Once a determination has been made as to the proper average weekly wage, the compensation rated, sometimes referred to as "comp" rated, is determined by multiplying the average weekly wage by 66 2/3 %. This comp rate equates to 2/3 of the employee's average weekly wage. However, in no event may the compensation rate be less than $30 per week.

There is a statutory ceiling on the amount of the compensation rate. No matter how high the employee's weekly wage, the comp rate may not exceed the maximum amount. The maximum workers' compensation rate is derived by multiplying North Carolina's average weekly insured wage by 1.10, and rounded such figure to the nearest multiple of $2.00. This maximum amount is determined specifically by the North Carolina Industrial Commission each year. For injuries occurring after January 1, 2008 the maximum weekly compensation rate is $786. For injuries occurring after January 1, 2007, the maximum weekly compensation rate is $754.00. For 2006, the maximum rate was $730.00; for 2005, the maximum rate was $704.00; for 2004, it was $688.00; for 2003, it was $674.00; and for 2002, it was $654.00.

Once the compensation rate has been correctly determined, it never changes. It does not increase as does social security disability benefits. It will stay the same no matter how many years the worker continues to receive workers' compensation benefits.

2. MEDICAL EXPENSES

The second major benefit, payment of all medical expenses, is probably the most valuable part of our workers' compensation benefits. Employers are 100% liable for all medical expenses incurred as a result of an on-the-job injury or illness. The law provides that employers must provide all reasonable medical, surgical, hospital, nursing and rehabilitation services, medicines, sick travel, and other treatment, including medical and surgical supplies as may be reasonably required to (a) effect a cure, (b) give relief (including relief from pain), or (c) lessen the period of disability.

The employer must also pay for artificial members (such as arms and legs) and for the replacement of such artificial members when reasonably necessary.

The law provides that no fees for medical expenses or medical services may be charged unless those fees are specifically approved by the Industrial Commission. In most cases, the Industrial Commission will not approve the full fees or charges imposed by the doctor, hospital, or other medical provider. However, the law specifically provides that the medical provider may not charge the employee for the unapproved balance of his fee. A medical provider who attempts to charge a worker with any part of a fee for medical services which has not been approved by the Industrial Commission is guilty of a criminal offense. Since the employer is liable for all of the charges for necessary medical expenses, the employee does not have to bear any of the cost for these necessary and approved medical expenses. Neither is the employee's health and hospital insurance carrier liable for these bills. This is important because most health insurance policies provide an exclusion for the payment of any medical or healthcare expenses resulting from an on-the-job injury or illness.

WHAT MEDICAL SERVICES MUST THE EMPLOYER PROVIDE?

The employer must provide all necessary and appropriate medical, surgical, hospital, or other treatment to the employee. Medical services which must be provided include physical therapy treatment, psychological therapy, chiropractic services, and attended care.

The law requires that such medical services shall be provided by the employer. In case of a controversy arising between the employer and employee relative to the continuation of medical, surgical, hospital or other treatment, the Industrial Commission may order such further treatment as may, in the discretion of the Industrial Commission, be necessary.

107

The character and amount of treatment appropriate for a particular employee is a matter which may only be decided by the Industrial Commission. The Industrial Commission may order such treatment or rehabilitation procedures that it determines, in its discretion, to be "reasonably necessary to effect a cure or give relief for an injured employee." So long as there is any evidence to support a decision by the Industrial Commission as to what type of medical care should be provided, the appellate courts will not disturb or interfere with a ruling of the Industrial Commission.

The court has approved a decision by the Industrial Commission requiring the employer to pay the injured worker's doctor for the cost of preparing a plan for future treatment of the injured worker for the remainder of his life.

The courts have ruled that the employer not only has an obligation to provide medical treatment which will lessen the period of disability, but must also pay for expenses which are reasonably required to effect a cure or give relief. The court defines the term "relief" to include not only an affirmative improvement towards an injured employee's health, but also the prevention or mitigation of further decline in that health due to the compensable injury. The court has defined "lessen the period of disability" to mean "lessen the period of time of diminution of earnings."

The employer is obligated to provide handicapped accessible housing to the worker when recommended by the doctor. This duty includes the requirement to pay for modification of the claimant's house to make it handicapped accessible.

The employer's obligation for medical services includes the requirement to pay for all medicines, sick travel, and medical and surgical supplies. The employer must provide for any

BRENT ADAMS

artificial limbs as may be reasonably necessary at the end of the healing period and must replace those artificial limbs when reasonably necessitated by ordinary use or medical circumstances.

The Industrial Commission has approved expenses for attendant care to the injured worker, including attendant care rendered by family members.

Employees are entitled to reimbursement for sick travel when travel is medically necessary and the round trip mileage to and from the medical providers is 20 miles or more. The per-mileage rate is set by the commission periodically.

Injured workers are entitled to lodging and meals when it is medically necessary for the employee to stay overnight at a location away from home. If an employee does not have a vehicle, the employer must pay the cost of a rental vehicle or the cost of the transportation when medically necessary. The worker is also entitled to reimbursement for the cost of parking.

See section 22 for discussion of the length of time during which medical expenses must be paid.

3. PAYMENT FOR PERMANENT IMPAIRMENT

The third major benefit of the workers' compensation law is the entitlement to payment for permanent impairments to one or more parts of the body. North Carolina law sets out specifically in rather a ghoulish cookbook fashion, the benefits available to the worker for impairment to his or her various body parts. The amount to be recovered for the loss of use of a body part is arrived at by a simple mathematical computation. For instance, if a worker should lose his thumb, he or she would be entitled to a sum for that loss equal to his

WORKERS' COMPENSATION IN NORTH CAROLINA

"comp rate," or two-thirds of his average weekly wage times 75 weeks. If a worker's average weekly wage was $300, the comp rate would be $200 (two-thirds of $300). For the loss of a thumb, the worker would be entitled to $15,000 ($200 x 75). This is far less than one would expect from a jury, were a jury to determine and assess the loss of a thumb over a person's lifetime in a trial in civil court.

It is not necessary that a body part be severed for there to be recovery for the total impairment of the body part. It is enough that the employee loses the use of the body part. For instance, the total paralysis of the thumb would be considered a "total loss" even though the thumb is not actually severed.

In most cases we deal with, there is not a total loss of use of the body part, but only partial. A common example deals with the back. The schedule of benefits set out by the law provides a payment for 300 weeks for total loss of use of the back. It is rare to have a total loss of the back. More frequently, what we see is a partial impairment of the back such as, for example, a loss of 10% use. To arrive at the benefit to be paid to the worker for a 10% loss of use of the back, one would multiply 300 weeks times 10%. The resulting 30 weeks would then be multiplied by the workers' compensation rate or two-thirds of the average weekly wage. In the case of a worker whose average weekly wage was $300, his comp rate would be $200, and this would be multiplied by 30 weeks to arrive at the sum of $6,000 to be paid for a 10% permanent loss of use of the back by this injured worker. Again, this is a figure much lower than we would expect from a North Carolina jury were these damages assessed outside the workers' compensation arena.

The degree of permanent impairment is assessed only at the end of the "healing period." This is determined after the worker has reached maximum medical improvement. In layman's terms, maximum medical improvement simply means that the worker's condition has healed as much as it will ever heal, and that the worker's condition will never improve above that level of maximum medical improvement. If the worker is not able to return to work even after the time he reaches maximum medical improvement, he will continue to receive his wage replacement benefits equal to two-thirds of his average weekly wage during the time he is out of work.

The benefit for permanent impairment to a part of the body is without regard to the worker's ability to earn wages. If, for example, a worker suffered a permanent partial impairment of a body part, but lost no wages and continued to work at his full salary (a very unlikely event), the worker would receive no salary continuation benefits, but would receive payment for the permanent partial impairment.

The extent of permanent impairment, sometimes referred to as the employee's "rating," is based upon the opinion of a physician determined by the rating guide published by the North Carolina Industrial Commission. Many times there are honest differences of opinion among physicians concerning the nature and extent of the worker's impairment. If a worker is dissatisfied with the rating given to him by a doctor, the worker is entitled to a second opinion by the doctor of his choice. The employer is responsible for paying all the cost of the second opinion.

If there is a dispute among physicians as to the correct impairment rating, that issue can be decided by the Industrial Commission at the request of either party. For instance, if one doctor gives a permanent impairment rating of 5% and another doctor gives an opinion of the impairment as 15%, the North Carolina Industrial Commission, sitting as a finder of the fact, will decide the correct rating. The Commission could either rule that the impairment is 5% or that the impairment is 15%, or that the impairment is somewhere in between. In many cases, the Industrial Commission averages the various ratings given by the doctors. However, this is not always the case and the Industrial Commission is free to agree with the opinion of any one doctor or can determine that the rate of impairment is somewhere between the rating given by any of the doctors.

The schedule of benefits for impairment of various body parts is set out below:

Thumb	75 weeks
Arm	240 weeks
First or index finger	45 weeks
Foot	144 weeks
Second or middle finger	40 weeks
Leg	200 weeks
Third or ring finger	25 weeks
Eye	120 weeks
Fourth or little finger	20 weeks
Hearing (one ear)	70 weeks
Great toe	35 weeks
Hearing (both ears)	150 weeks
Any other toe	10 weeks
Back	300 weeks
Hand	200 weeks

THE TRAGIC EXCEPTION

If a worker loses both hands, both arms, both feet, both legs, or both eyes (or any *two* of these body parts), the worker is considered to be totally and permanently disabled. This worker would then be entitled to 2/3 of his average weekly

wage for the rest of his life. These benefits continue even if
the tragically injured employee is able to return to work, no
matter what level of income he is able to earn. Even though
this is the most beneficial remedy for any employee, it is
small compensation indeed for what the worker has given up
for his employer.

HERNIAS

Hernias which arise from an accident or a specific traumatic
incident of the work assigned to the employee are also
compensable. There are certain special requirements,
however, in order to recover for a hernia. In order to recover,
the worker must prove: (a) that there was an injury resulting
in hernia or rupture; (b) that the hernia or rupture appeared
suddenly; (c) that the hernia or rupture immediately followed
an accident or a specific traumatic incident; and (d) that the
hernia or rupture did not exist prior to the accident or specific
traumatic incident for which compensation is claimed.

COMPENSATION FOR OTHER BODY PARTS
OR ORGANS

In the case of the loss of, or a permanent injury to all or any
part of any important external or internal organ or part of the
body for which the rate of compensation is not set out above,
the Industrial Commission may award compensation up to
$20,000 for such loss. The $20,000 limit is for each specific
body part or organ. If there is permanent total or partial
impairment to more than one organ or body part, the loss to
each body part should be computed, and the total amount can
be more than $20,000 provided that the amount for each body
part or organ is no greater than $20,000.

In making these awards, the amount of the award, if any, for
loss to an additional body part not set out above or for loss to

organs, at the discretion of the Industrial Commission. It may award a figure in its discretion up to the limit or may award nothing. Although neither the statutes nor the opinions of our appellate courts have stated that earning capacity can be considered in determining an award for loss of use of unnamed body parts or organs, two appellate court decisions seem to support such a holding. An employee is not required to establish a diminution of wage earning capacity in order to be entitled to compensation for loss resulting from impairment of unnamed body parts or organs. However, such lost earning capacity may be considered in setting the amount of the award. Examples of other body parts or organs for which compensation has been awarded include loss of the sense of taste or smell, sinuses, nerves and muscles of the face ($20,000); the pancreas ($20,000); the lungs ($20,000 each / total for two $40,000); abdominal wall ($15,000); the omentum ($10,000); intestines ($12,000); stomach ($5,000); reproductive organs ($15,000); the uterus ($15,000); the bladder ($11,000) and the spleen ($20,000).

HEARING LOSS

If hearing loss is caused by an accidental injury, the worker can recover 70 weeks of workers' compensation benefits for total loss of hearing in one ear and 150 weeks of benefits for total hearing loss in both ears. If loss of hearing by injury from an accident is only partial, recovery will be limited to such portion of those periods of payment as such partial loss becomes total loss.

If hearing loss is caused by sustained loud noise levels at work, it will be considered an occupational disease. There is a special set of rules which deals exclusively with hearing loss. As a general rule, if a worker suffers a permanent sensorineural loss of hearing in both ears caused by prolonged exposure to harmful noise in employment, he can recover 150 weeks of compensation (2/3 of the workers' average weekly wage multiplied by 150.) For partial loss of hearing in both ears, recovery is limited to such portion of this period of payment as such partial loss bears to total loss.

If the worker had a partial hearing loss before taking the job, the employer is only liable for the difference between the hearing loss as of the date of disability and the percent of hearing loss existing before the claimant first started working for the employer.

No claims for hearing loss can be made until six months after the last exposure to the harmful noise.

No recovery may be had if the worker fails to use employer – provided protection devices capable of preventing loss of hearing from harmful noise.

For occupational hearing loss, no compensation will be paid unless there is a loss of hearing in both ears. An exception is made in those cases in which the worker had a pre-existing deafness in one ear due to disease, trauma, or congenital deafness. In that case the worker can recover for loss of hearing for his one previously good ear starting at the rate of 70 weeks of compensation for total occupational loss of hearing.

AN ALTERNATE WAY TO DETERMINE COMPENSATION FOR PERMANENT PARTIAL IMPAIRMENT TO THE BODY

In cases in which the employee has a permanent impairment to one or more of the parts of his body and can earn wages in some amount but is unable to earn wages which are as great as was earned before the injury, the employee, rather than choosing the benefits for permanent impairment of a body part under the schedule set out above, may elect to be compensated based upon another formula. He may elect instead to receive 2/3 of the wage difference between what the worker was earning before his injury, and what he is able to earn after the injury. For instance, if the worker earned $700 per week after the injury, but because of his injury or illness could only return to work and be paid a rate of $400 per week, he could elect to be paid based upon the difference between the two figures. In that case, the difference would be $300 per week and the worker would be entitled to 2/3 of that amount or $200 per week. The problem with this alternative is that the statute limits recovery under this provision to a period of no greater than 300 weeks from the date of the injury. In addition, if the worker received workers' compensation benefits for his total but temporary disability before returning to work, those weeks count against the worker and reduce the 300 week (wage replacement) period.

Additionally, if the worker earns raises during this period, such a raise would result in a corresponding reduction in workers' compensation benefits.

This alternative method of computing entitlement for permanent impairment is usually not as beneficial to the worker as electing to take benefits based upon the schedule of impairments listed above. However, there are cases in which the alternative method is more beneficial. The issue has to be decided on a case per case basis with special attention to the probable events which may occur in the future. Of course, the future is always difficult to predict, and great care should be taken when making this election.

The election of which method to compute payment for permanent impairment does not arise, however, until the worker has reached maximum medical improvement and has returned to work. Unfortunately, in many cases, the worker is never able to return to work in any capacity. In that case, the worker will continue to receive wage replacement benefits at the rate of 2/3 of the workers' average weekly wage for the rest of his life.

PERMANENT BACK INJURIES

In cases in which there is a 75% or more loss of use of the back, the injured worker shall be deemed to have suffered "total industrial disability" and will be compensated for a total loss of use of the back. In this case, the worker will receive his compensation rate for the rest of his life or until he is able to find "suitable" employment earning the same or greater wages as he was earning at the time of his injury.

PERMANENT AND TOTAL IMPAIRMENT

If the worker's impairment is permanent and total, he is entitled to two-third's of his average weekly wage for every week of the remainder of his life.

4. BENEFITS FOR DISFIGUREMENT

A worker may be compensated for injuries which leave "serious" facial or head scars. Unfortunately, the limit of benefits available for serious facial and head disfigurement is limited to $20,000.

If there is "serious" bodily disfigurement, as opposed to disfigurement of the face or head, the employee may recover for such disfigurement a sum up to $10,000. The claimant must also show that such disfigurement hampers his ability to find employment. What constitutes "serious" bodily disfigurement is within the discretion of the Industrial Commission. Scars on the knees or arms have been compensated by the Industrial Commission, but such scars, particularly on a male, do not usually result in a significant recovery. However, it is usually worth the effort to try to recover for any scars or disfigurement if the worker feels they are significant.

In the case of both facial and head disfigurement, as well as bodily disfigurement, if there is not an agreement between the employee and the employer or its insurance carrier, the issue of the amount of disfigurement will be decided by the Industrial Commission which will examine the claimant personally or by way of photographs to determine what the Commission feels is appropriate compensation for the disfigurement, subject to the statutory limits mentioned above.

In the case of the loss of an eye, when an artificial eye cannot be fitted and used, the Industrial Commission may consider that a serious facial disfigurement and may award up to $20,000.

There is another limitation to the amount of compensation that can be awarded for bodily disfigurement. If the disfigurement resulted from the permanent loss, or a permanent partial loss of the use of any member of the body for which compensation is paid under the provisions set out above, no additional amount may be paid for the disfigurement associated with the permanent or partial loss for that part of the body. For instance, if a worker loses a leg and is compensated for that loss based upon 200 weeks of

workers' compensation benefits as set out above, that worker
cannot recover anything additionally for the disfigurement
resulting from the loss of his leg.

Our appellate courts have held that separate awards must be
made in cases involving facial disfigurement and bodily
disfigurement. If a worker has become disfigured in his face
and his body as a result of a work-related injury, the worker
is entitled to recovery from both of these disfigurements. The
limit on the bodily disfigurement is $10,000, whereas the
limit for the facial disfigurement is $20,000. Therefore,
theoretically, a worker could be awarded a total of $30,000
for disfigurement of the face and body.

The courts have ruled that in order to be payable, a
disfigurement must not only be a "marked" disfigurement,
but also one which impairs the future occupational
opportunity of the injured employee.

One court has ruled that in order to be compensable, the
disfigurement must be so permanent and serious that in some
manner it hampers or handicaps the person in his earnings or
in securing employment, or it must be such as to make the
person repulsive to other people. This case seems to stand,
therefore, for the proposition that a disfigurement may be
compensable even if there is no impairment of earning
capacity. Indeed, the Industrial Commission has frequently
awarded compensation for disfigurement when there is no
proof that the disfigurement impaired earning capacity.

The law gives the Industrial Commission the discretion as to
whether to award anything for serious bodily disfigurement.
On the other hand with respect to serious facial or head
disfigurement, the law provides that the Commission "shall
award proper and equitable compensation not to exceed

$20,000." The courts have ruled that this statute makes it mandatory on the Commission to award fair and equitable compensation in the case of serious facial or head disfigurement. However, that is not the case with regard to disfigurement of other parts of the body.

One appellate court decision has ruled that in compensation for serious disfigurement, the Commission should consider "the natural physical handicap resulting and the age, training, experience, education, occupation, and adaptability of the employee to obtain and retain employment."

In the case in which an employee is found to have a total and permanent disability, no additional compensation is allowed for disfigurement, serious or otherwise.

5. PAYMENT OF DEATH BENEFITS

If a worker dies from an on-the-job injury, his or her family is entitled to substantial benefits.

In order for the family to qualify for benefits, the employee must have died within six years from an on-the-job accident or occupational disease *or* within two years from the final determination of the disability, whichever is later. This claim must be filed within two years of the day of death. The claim should be filed by the dependents or next of kin of the decedent employee. The claim cannot be filed by the estate of the deceased employee. Compensation payments due as a result of the death of the injured worker shall be paid for a period of 400 weeks from the death. However, compensation payments will continue to be paid to a widow or a widower after the 400 weeks provided that, as of the date of the worker's death, the widow or widower was unable to support himself or herself because of physical or mental disability. If such a disability exists, compensation payments will be paid during the remainder of the lifetime of the widow or widower or until their remarriage. Compensation payments made to a minor child shall continue until the child reaches the age of 18 even if that time span is in excess of 400 weeks.

A widow or widower and a child or children are conclusively presumed to be wholly dependent upon the deceased worker. If there is more than one person wholly dependent upon the deceased worker, those benefits would be divided equally among all of the dependents. For instance, if a deceased worker is survived by a widow and two minor children the total monthly comp benefits will be divided equally among them.

If there is a decrease in the dependent beneficiary pool during the 400 weeks following the employee's death, there must be a corresponding reapportionment of the full amount payable for that set period among the remaining eligible members of the pool. For instance, in the example set out above when each of the children becomes 18 years of age he is no longer beneficiary of the death benefit. At that point, the weekly compensation rate will be divided among the remaining minor children and the widow. When all the children become 18 years of age, providing the 400 weeks have not totally elapsed, the widow would be the only beneficiary and would therefore be entitled to the entire payment.

The weekly compensation rate in the case of death is the same as would be payable to the employee had he survived. That amount is two-thirds of the average weekly wage, but not more than the maximum amount set by statute or less than $30.00 per week.

6. TRAVEL EXPENSES FOR MEDICAL TREATMENT

The injured worker is entitled to be paid for expenses incurred in traveling to the doctor or other medical or healthcare providers. If the distance required to travel to the medical providers is 20 miles or more roundtrip, the employer has to reimburse the employee mileage charges for necessary travel for medical care. The Industrial Commission periodically sets the mileage rate. Currently, the rate is 44.5 cents per mile.

7. HOUSING ACCMMODATIONS AND MEALS NECESSARY FOR MEDICAL TREATMENT

When it is necessary for the injured employee to travel away from his home in order to receive medical care, the employer is required to pay for lodging accommodations and meals which are incurred in connection with travel for medical care.

The injured employee is also entitled to reimbursement for the costs of parking incurred in connection with the necessary medical care. The rate for lodging and meal expenses is set by the Industrial Commission and is adjusted periodically.

8. MODIFICATION OF RESIDENCE

In those cases in which; an injury or occupational disease necessitates the use of a wheelchair by the injured employee, the employer could be required to pay for modifications to the claimant's residence so as to make the residence wheelchair accessible. In addition, the Industrial Commission may order the employer and its insurance carrier to pay any other costs for modifications to the injured worker's home which are deemed necessary as a result of the physical limitations of the worker.

9. ATTORNEY'S FEES

As a general rule, the injured worker cannot require the employer or its insurance carrier to pay attorney's fees.

If, after the initial hearing before a Deputy Commissioner, the employer or its insurance carrier appeals the decision of the Deputy Commissioner to the Full Industrial Commission, the Industrial Commission may, in its discretion, order that the employer or its insurance company pay attorney's fees to the employee's attorney.

If the Industrial Commission finds that any hearing or motion has been brought or that the case was defended without reasonable grounds, it may order the party who brought the hearing or motion or raised the defense, which was not based upon reasonable grounds, to pay attorney's fees. This provision of the law works both ways. If the Industrial Commission finds that the employee brought an action without reasonable grounds, the employee could be ordered to pay the attorney's fees to the employer or its insurance carrier. If the Industrial Commission finds that the employee's claim was defended without a reasonable basis, the Industrial Commission could order the employer and its insurance carrier to pay the employee's attorney's fees.

In both of the situations described above, the decision to award attorney's fees is totally in the discretion of the Industrial Commission. The appellate courts will not reverse this decision by the Industrial Commission unless the appellate courts find that the Industrial Commission abused its discretion. It would be most unusual for the appellate courts to make such a finding.

The Industrial Commission very rarely awards attorney's fees to either party. Therefore, you should assume that in your case, you will have to pay your attorney's fees and the employer and its insurance carrier will pay their attorney's fees.

All attorney's fees charged to the employee must first be approved by the Industrial Commission.

Most lawyers who do workers' compensation work are willing to represent employees on a contingency fee basis. Under this arrangement, the employee does not owe attorney's fees unless there is a recovery. The customary contingency fee rate is 25% of the total recovery, subject to the approval of the North Carolina Industrial Commission. Some lawyers charge more than 25%. Many lawyers charge a higher percentage if there is an appeal either to the Full Industrial Commission or to the Appellate Courts.

SECTION 14
EVENTS FOR WHICH WORKERS'
COMPENSATION BENEFITS MAY BE
PAYABLE

Employees are entitled to workers' compensation benefits if, while carrying out the duties of their employment, they: (1) suffer an injury by accident, (2) suffer a "specific traumatic incident resulting in a hernia or an injury to the back; or (3) develop an occupational disease."

1. SUFFER AN INJURY BY ACCIDENT

WHAT IS AN ACCIDENT?

The term "injury by accident" has a very specific meaning in the workers' compensation law. Cases are won and lost simply upon the issue of whether an occurrence was an "injury by accident" under the North Carolina Workers' Compensation Act. The term "injury" means only an injury by accident arising out of and in the course of the employment. The term does not include a disease in any form except for such disease which result naturally and unavoidably from the accident. Injury also includes the breakage or damage to eyeglasses, hearing aids, dentures, or other prosthetic devices which function as part of the body.

An injury, to be payable, must result from an accident. This accident is to be considered as a separate event preceding and causing the injury. The mere fact of an injury does not in and of itself establish the fact of an accident.

Our courts have defined "accident" in various ways. One definition is that an accident is "an unlooked for and untoward event which is not expected or designed by the injured employee." Another court opinion states that an accident is "an unusual and unexpected fortuitous occurrence."

An event that involves both an employee's normal work routine and normal working conditions will not be considered to have been caused by accident. If the employee is performing his or her regular duties in the usual and customary manner, and is injured, there is no "accident," and the injury is not compensable.

It is not always easy to predict how the court will rule on whether a specific event was an accident. The facts of each case are different, and some of the decisions of the court seem inconsistent.

An accident which involves the interruption of the workers' normal work routine and the introduction thereby of unusual conditions is likely to result in unexpected consequences, and injuries arising therefrom will be considered to be an "injury by accident." On the other hand, once an activity even strenuous or otherwise unusual, becomes a part of the employee's normal work routine, an injury caused by such activity is not the result of the interruption of the work routine and is not considered to be an "injury by accident." One case has held that no matter how great the injury, if it is caused by an event that involves both the employee's normal work routine and normal working conditions, it would not be considered an accident.

A worker who trips or loses his or her balance while carrying out the ordinary responsibilities of his job in the usual way would, however, be entitled to benefits since this tripping or a loss of balance turns the event into an "accident." Without the fall or tripping, however, that same employee doing his job in the usual and customary way would not be entitled to benefits. Ordinarily, death from heart disease is not an injury by accident arising out of and in the course of employment so as to be compensable. On the other hand, our appellate courts have said that damage to the heart tissue clearly precipitated or caused by "over-exertion" constitutes an injury by accident.

In another case, the court held that evidence that the room temperature in the nuclear power plant was 85 degrees, and that the worker suffered heat exhaustion while wearing a radiation suit which inhibited his body's ability to radiate heat unequivocally demonstrated that the worker was exposed to an increased risk of heart-related illnesses because of his equipment. The worker's subsequent cardiac arrest was a "compensable accident."

Where a carpenter who was hired to perform a number of tasks connected with his employer's home improvement business was injured when he shifted his position while shingling a roof, the court deemed that that event occurred under normal work conditions and was not compensable as an injury suffered as a result of an accident.

Issues involving whether an injury resulted from an accident are usually complex. Therefore, the assistance of a skilled and experienced workers' compensation lawyer should be utilized to help the injured worker resolve these issues.

The requirement that an injury results "from an accident" no longer applies with respect to hernias and injuries occurring to the back.

FALLS

It seems obvious that a fall at work would be considered an accident. In most cases falls are considered to be compensable. However, as in most areas of the law, there are exceptions.

The general rule concerning fall cases is that where the injury is clearly attributable to an unknown condition of the employee, with no factors intervening or operating to cause or contribute to the injury, there will be no recovery. However, where the injury is associated with any risk attributable to the employment, compensation should be allowed even though the employee may have suffered from an unknown condition which precipitated or contributed to the injury.

The following are examples of fall cases which have been held not to be compensable:

(1) An injured worker got into his car to leave the defendant's plant. The night watchman, however, called the worker to come to him; and, in getting out of the car to learn what the watchman wanted, the injured worker slipped on a fruit peeling. The court denied the claim, writing that: "When an injury cannot fairly be traced to the employment as a contributing proximate cause, or comes from a hazard to which the worker would be equally exposed apart from employment or from a hazard to others, it does not arise out of the employment." This is a 1938 case and probably would not be followed today. Certainly, it should not be followed.

(2) In a case in which the injured worker fell after his leg (for no apparent reason) gave way, the court held that there would be no recovery.

(3) An injured worker was subject to epileptic fits, and while driving his employer's truck, felt a seizure approaching. The worker stopped the truck on the side of the road, after which he suffered an epileptic seizure and lost consciousness. When he came to, his body was on the outside of the truck and his hands were on the steering wheel. He had suffered broken bones caused by the fall from the seat of the truck. The court denied benefits for the injured worker and held that the evidence disclosed that the sole cause of the fall from the truck was the epileptic seizure, and that it was therefore independent and unrelated to the employment.

HORSEPLAY

The courts have generally held that injuries arising from the gathering together of workers of various characteristics, and the risks and hazards of such close contact, including joking and pranks by the workers, are incident to the business and grow out of it and are ordinarily risks assumed by the employer. Therefore, as a general rule, workers injured as a result of horseplay engaged in by employees are generally considered to be payable, and the worker can recover for these injuries. This is true even though the horseplay was initiated and participated in by the injured worker.

ASSAULTS AT WORK

Although an assault is an intentional act, it may be considered an accident within the meaning of the workers' compensation law when it is unexpected and without design on the part of the employee victim.

When a disagreement arises out of work and a worker is assaulted, it is usually held that such an assault grows out of the employment and is therefore compensable. However, the danger which causes the assault must be peculiar to the work and not common to the neighborhood. It must be incidental to the character of the business and not independent of the relation of worker and employee.

The assault need not have been foreseen or expected, but after the event, it must appear to have had its origin or risk connected with the employment and to have flowed from that source as a rational consequence.

Where the assault upon the employee grows out of a motive foreign to the employment relationship, the necessary connection between the injury and the employment is not presented, and there will be no compensation awarded for the injury.

When the cause of an assault upon an employee by a third person is personal, or when the circumstances surrounding the assault furnishes no basis for a reasonable inference that the nature of the employment created a risk of such an attack, the injury is not payable. This is true even though the employee was engaged in the performance of its duties at the time.

The courts have held that the risk of murder by a jealous spouse is not an incident of employment. This is true even though there was a possibility that the employee's spouse became jealous of an associate at work.

The courts held that this is a hazard common to the neighborhood, is independent of the relationship of employer/employee, and is not a risk arising out of the employment.

In one case an employee was struck with a shovel by a co-employee after he had spoken words to him which he deemed insulting. The attacking worker left he place of employment, returned, and struck the other worker causing permanent injury. The court held that there was evidence of "injury by accident arising out of and in the course of the employment," and the claim therefore was payable.

When a worker was shot in the eye by a hunter while working on his employer's truck, the court held that the injury did not result from a cause peculiar to the employment in which the worker was engaged, and therefore it was not compensable. On the other hand, in another case the court held that when an employee whose duty it was to collect accounts for his employer was struck and killed by a debtor of his employer the evidence was sufficient to support a finding that the death was a result of an accident arising out of and in the course of employment.

A game warden was killed by a person against whom he had testified in a criminal action for violation of the game law; the court held that the injury did not arise out of and in the course of the employment for the State.

Where a delivery man was driving a truck in the course of his employment, and while passing a group of boys playing baseball, a baseball struck his windshield and injured him. The court held that that injury resulted from an accident arising out of and in the course and scope of employment.

As can be seen from the examples set out above, the rulings of the court on the issue of whether an injury arose out of and in the course and scope of employment are somewhat inconsistent. It is doubtful whether all the cases cited above would be decided the same way were they heard today.

Because of the difficulty of predicting whether the courts will hold that accidents are compensable in certain unusual fact situations, it is always important to retain an experienced workers' compensation attorney to help resolve these matters.

STORM AND WEATHER RELATED INJURIES

North Carolina courts have been rather inconsistent in ruling upon injuries that occur from accidents related to weather conditions.

As a general rule, where the employment subjects a worker to a special or a particular hazard from the elements such as excessive cold or heat, likely to produce sun stroke or freezing, death or disability resulting from such causes usually are payable. On the other hand, where the employee is not by reason of his work peculiarly exposed to an injury by sun stroke or freezing, such injuries are not ordinarily compensable. The test is whether the employment subjects the worker to a greater hazard or risk than that to which the worker would otherwise be exposed.

A bus driver was compelled to change a tire on the defendant's bus during very cold weather and contracted pneumonia. The worker was denied workers' compensation benefits.

In another case, the worker was in the employer's plant when he was struck by a tornado which caused a partial collapse of the building. The court held that the worker could not collect for his injuries which directly resulted from the partial collapse of the building. According to the court, there was no causal or connection between the employment and the accident.

The court has ruled that there could be recovery in a case of the death of an employee from heat exhaustion or sun stroke. The evidence was that the temperature outside was 104 degrees, and the employee's work required that he be in close proximity to melted lead, which increased the temperature in the building where the employees was working on the day of his death.

A carpenter caught in a storm while working was struck by lightning when he went to a nearby house under construction by his employer to get out of the rain. The court found that there was sufficient evidence to support the conclusion that the circumstances of the carpenter's employment peculiarly exposed him to the risk of injury from lightning greater than that of others in the community. Among the factors which the court considered were the following: (a) The worker wearing wet clothes, was standing near a window talking with his employer; (b) He was wearing a carpenter's nail apron with nails therein; (c) All damage to the worker's clothes and marks on the body were from the waist down; (d) The nail apron was knocked off his body; (e) A hole was burned in the nail apron; and (f) A majority of the nails in the nail apron were fused.

SUICIDE

No workers' compensation benefits can be collected for the death of a worker if that death was intentionally caused by the worker. In most cases, therefore, there can be no recovery of workers' compensation benefits resulting from suicide.

In those cases where the injuries suffered by the injured employee result in his losing normal judgment and becoming dominated by a disturbance of mind directly caused by his work-related injury and its consequences, his suicide cannot be considered "willful" and, therefore, his family can claim workers' compensation benefits for his death.

The law provides that a suicide cannot be intentional if it results from a mental condition resulting from the work-related injury and the worker is unable to control the impulse to kill himself.

If the suicide is not "willful," the suicide will not bar recovery for the deceased workers' family.

THE ACCIDENT MUST OCCUR WHILE AT WORK

To state that a worker must be injured while at work in order to recover for a workers' compensation injury seems too obvious a statement to require mentioning. However, many cases rise and fall upon whether the injured worker was "at work" at the time of the injury.

The legal term for this requirement is that the accident in which the worker was injured must "arise out of and in the course of employment." The employee must be engaged in some activity or duty which he is authorized to undertake and which is calculated to further, directly or indirectly, the employer's business.

While this requirement seems obvious, there are many factual occurrences which make it difficult to determine whether the accident meets the legal requirement of being "out of and in the course of employment." If it does not meet the legal requirement, the worker cannot recover no matter how severe the injury.

To be payable under the Workers' Compensation Act, an injury must arise out of and be received in the course of employment. Two ideas are involved here. The words "in the course of" refer to the time, place and circumstances surrounding the accident, while the words "arising out of" have reference to the causal connection between the injury and the employment. The courts have said the manner in which the injury occurred or the phrase "arising out of and in the course of employment" ·encompass two separate and distinct concepts: "out of" and "in the course of," both of which must be satisfied in order for particular injuries to be held compensable under the Act.

An injury arises out of employment when it is a natural and probable consequence of the employment and the natural result of risks inherent with such employment, so that there is some causal relationship between the employment and the injury.

A cocktail waitress sustained injuries when she tried to escape from a guest of the resort who had kidnapped and sexually assaulted her. Here injuries arose out of and in the course and scope of her employment, even though the attack occurred after the employee's workday ended when she stopped on a resort road to assist a guest, who she assumed had car trouble.

When an cmployce was injured by accident while riding in a truck on a vacation pleasure trip which was provided and paid for by his employer as a matter of good will and personnel relations among employees, that injury is held not to be within the course and scope of the employment and therefore not compensable.

When an employee was injured while attending a goodwill picnic at the invitation of the employer, the court held that that injury was not compensable, because the employee did no work and was not paid for attendance, nor penalized for nonattendance. On the other hand, in another case where an employee injured her ankle while dancing at an annual

Christmas party sponsored and paid for by her employer, where wages were paid for the time the employee spent at the party, and where the plant manager considered the party an employee fringe benefit, the court held that that injury was compensable.

THE GOING AND COMING RULE

One common situation is when the worker is injured while traveling to and from work. The general rule in that situation is that there is no payment for the injured worker if he or she is injured while traveling to work or traveling home from work. However, there are many exceptions.

One exception is known as the "premises exception" to the "going and coming" rule which holds that injuries arising on the premises of the employer, such as in a parking lot, would be compensable even though the worker was injured while going to work.

Another exception is the traveling salesman exception which covers workers who are required to travel from place to place as, for instance, a route salesman. In those cases, traveling workers can collect even though they are on the first leg of their trip, traveling to their first appointment, or on the last leg traveling home from their last appointment.

The "special errand" exception provides that an injury is in the course of the employment if it occurs while the employee is engaged in a special duty or a special errand away from the usual job site. An example is that of a worker who was required, as a condition of employment, to attend a four-week training seminar which was not offered at his regular place of employment. When the worker was injured while traveling to this training seminar, the court held that the injury arose within the course of employment, and the worker collected for his injuries.

One worker was injured on his way to work while crossing the street to purchase supplies for the school where he worked at the specific request of the principal. It was held that the worker was on a special errand for his employer and the injuries sustained while crossing the street were payable.

Injuries arising out of the necessity of sleeping in hotels or eating in restaurants away from home are usually held to be payable. When a traveling worker slips in the street or is struck by an automobile between his hotel and a restaurant, the injury has been held to be payable even though the accident occurred on a Sunday evening and involved an extended trip occasioned by the employee's wish to eat at a particular restaurant. In general, if the employer creates the necessity for travel, that travel is considered to be in the course of his employment even though he is serving at the same time some purpose of his own. However, injuries received while on a trip being made primarily for personal or social reasons and not in performance of his duty for the employer, is not payable, even if the employer has also benefited from the trip. An example of this rule arose in a case involving a worker who was killed when he went with another to visit the other person's girlfriend, and while on the visit stopped to get supplies for his employer. That accident was held not to be within the course of his employment, and therefore, there was no recovery for the death which occurred to the employee.

The employer may be held liable for an injury suffered by an employee when going to or from work when the employer furnishes the means of transportation as a part of the contract of employment. An injury suffered by an employee while going to or from work is considered to have arisen out of and in the course of his employment when the employee, under the terms of the employment, and as an incident of the contract, is paid an allowance to cover the cost of such transportation. This rule applies even when the employee is traveling to and from lunch on a vehicle furnished by the employer.

The North Carolina Court of Appeals recently created another exception to the going and coming rule when it held that if the employer required the employee to provide the means for transportation to use while at work, the employer is liable to pay workers' compensation benefits to that worker if he is injured while traveling to or from work. This exception would arise, for instance, if a worker was required to drive his car while at work. If the employee is in an accident while driving this car to work, he can claim workers' compensation benefits for injuries sustained in the accident even though he had not yet arrived at his job site when the accident happened.

ACCIDENTS WHICH OCCUR OUTSIDE THE STATE

It is not necessary that an accident occur within the state of North Carolina in order for the injured worker to collect workers' compensation benefits under North Carolina law. Neither is it a requirement that the injured employee be a resident of North Carolina.

In order to recover for an injury that occurs outside the state of North Carolina the employee must meet one of the following requirements:
- The contract of employment was made in North Carolina,
- The employer's principal place of business is in North Carolina,

- The employee's principal place of employment is within the state of North Carolina.

If the employee who is injured outside the state of North Carolina receives compensation or damages under the laws of any other state, North Carolina will not allow further benefits under North Carolina's Workers' compensation Act, if such payment, together with the payment received from other jurisdictions, would amount to greater than the benefits allowed under North Carolina law for a worker injured in this state.

The North Carolina Court of Appeals has held that a truck driver who made 18-20% of his pick up stops in North Carolina and the balance of his pick ups being made in other states was entitled to full workers' compensation benefits for injuries arising from an accident which occurred outside the state. The basis for the court's holding was the finding by the Industrial Commission that the driver's principal place of employment was within North Carolina. Also supporting the claim was the fact that the employee was a resident of North Carolina and conducted various aspects of his business including the receipt of assignments, storage and maintenance of trucks, receipt of paychecks, etc. in North Carolina.

2. SPECIFIC TRAUMATIC INCIDENT "RESULTING IN A HERNIA OR BACK INJURY."

It is apparent from the previous discussion concerning "injury by accident" that many of the court decisions are harsh and result in a denial of benefits to deserving employees. This is especially true with respect to workers doing hard physical labor who experience back injuries while carrying on the usual and customary duties for his employer in the usual way.

In recognizing this unfairness to the employee, the North Carolina General Assembly in 1983 added the following to the statutory definition of injury: "With respect to back injuries, however, where injury to the back arises out of and in the course of the employment and is the direct result of a specific traumatic incident of the work assigned, 'injury by accident' shall be construed to include any disabling physical injury to the back arising out of and causally related to such incident."

As a result of this very significant amendment to the law, workers who injure their back at work while performing the ordinary and usual duties of their job can now recover workers' compensation benefits for back injuries. Prior to this amendment to the law, these unfortunate injured workers could not recover anything though they had been seriously disabled while working.

A common example of the kind of injury which is now compensable, but which was not compensable before the amendment, is a case of a brick layer who stoops down to pick up a load of bricks, and his back "goes out on him." Before the amendment, that injured brick layer would not recover. Now, with the amendment to the statute, this event would clearly be compensable as a specific traumatic incident.

A "specific traumatic incident" need not involve unusual conditions or a departure from the worker's normal work routine.

Although the law with respect to back injuries has been amended to include more injured workers, there must still be evidence that the specific traumatic incident "caused" injury to the back. In addition, there must be evidence that the injury from the specific traumatic incident occurred within a relevant time period.

The law still requires that the specific traumatic incident resulting in back injury arise out of and in the course and scope of the injured workers' employment.

It is not necessary that the back injury and the pain occur simultaneously. Just because a claimant felt pain for the first time hours after he injured his back did not mean the "specific traumatic incident" could not have occurred when he said that it did.

3. OCCUPATIONAL DISEASES:

Workers can also recover under North Carolina Workers' Compensation Act if they become ill and are rendered unable to work as a result of an occupational disease.

The North Carolina Supreme Court has defined an occupational disease as "a diseased condition caused by a series of events, of a similar or like nature, occurring regularly or at frequent intervals over an extended period of time in employment." The Supreme Court also accepted the following definition of occupational disease: "A diseased condition arising gradually from the character of the employees work."

By statute in North Carolina occupational diseases are "treated as the happening of an injury by accident within the meaning of the North Carolina Workers' Compensation Act and the procedure and practice and compensation and other benefits provided by said act shall apply in all such cases..."

The North Carolina General Assembly has listed diseases which are to be deemed occupational diseases. Among these are the following:

- Anthrax poisoning
- Arsenic poisoning
- Brass poisoning
- Zinc poisoning
- Manganese poisoning
- Lead poisoning
- Mercury poisoning
- Phosphorus poisoning
- Poisoning by carbon bisulphide, menthanol, naphtha or volatile halogenated hydrocarbons
- Chrome ulceration
- Compressed-air illness
- Poisoning by benzol, or by nitro and amido derivatives of benzol, aniline, and others.
- Epitheliomatous cancer or ulceration of the skin.
- Radium poisoning.
- Blisters due to use of tools or appliances in the employment
- Bursitis
- Miner's nystagmus
- Bone felon
- Synovitis
- Tenosynovitis
- Carbon monoxide poisoning
- Poisoning by sulphuric, hydrochloric or hydrofluoric acid
- Asbestosis
- Silicosis
- Psittacosis
- Undulant fever
- Infection with smallpox, infection with vaccinia, or any adverse medical reaction when the infection or adverse reaction is due to the employee receiving in employment vaccination against smallpox or due to the employee being exposed to another employee vaccinated as described.

EXPOSURE TO A GREATER RISK OF HARM
(A CATCH-ALL PROVISION)

An employee is entitled to workers' compensation benefits
for disability caused by a condition to which the employment
specifically contributed, if the employment exposed the
worker to a greater risk of contracting the disease than existed
for the public in general.

When we think about occupational diseases, those conditions
resulting from cotton dust, coal dust, and asbestos usually
come to mind. There are specific statutes dealing with these
conditions. These statutes are very complex and will not be
dealt with in this book. If your loved one has been damaged
by exposure to cotton dust, coal dust, or asbestos, you should
contact an experienced workers' compensation lawyer
immediately since, as with all areas of workers'
compensation, there are specific deadlines which must be
observed. Otherwise the claim can be lost forever.

North Carolina statutory law contains a catch-all provision
which includes as an occupational disease "any disease...
which is proven to be due to causes and conditions which are
characteristic of and peculiar to a particular trade, occupation
or employment, but excluding all ordinary diseases of life to
which the general public is equally exposed outside the
employment."

This catch all provision has opened up for possible receipt of
benefits all sorts of conditions which were previously not
covered by the Workers' Compensation Law and were
therefore not previously compensable.

Chief among these new compensable conditions are those
caused by repetitive motion. One of the most common

repetitive motion diseases is carpal tunnel syndrome caused by the repetitive typing on a computer keyboard. Many cases have held that a worker may recover full workers' compensation benefits for carpal tunnel syndrome caused by repetitive motion.

If the worker can prove that: (1) His or her work environment placed him/her at a greater risk of developing carpal tunnel syndrome than exists for members of the public in general; and (2) The work environment was a significant contributing factor to contracting carpal tunnel syndrome, that worker would be entitled to full workers' compensation benefits.

This catch-all provision makes it possible to recover for any conceivable exposure at the workplace which results in adverse consequences to the employee requiring healthcare or inability to work.

Carpal tunnel syndrome is an example of a repetitive movement disease. There are many other repetitive movement diseases arising out of the workplace. One specific example handled by the author's law firm involved a man whose only job was to paste labels on tires. He was required to flip his wrist each time he placed a label on a tire. He placed labels on literally thousands of these tires a day.

Another example which was handled by the author's law firm involved a man who worked for a meat processing plant. His only job was to use a machete to cut the heads off hog carcasses as they passed through an assembly line. Three or four strokes were required to completely sever the hog's head. This worker, along with a co-worker who stood opposite him on the assembly line, severed several thousand heads a day during the normal work schedule. This man worked the same job for many years and, as a result, developed a very serious condition which rendered him totally and permanently disabled. The Industrial Commission held that this was an occupational disease caused by repetitive movements required at his work.

Recently the Industrial Commission and the North Carolina Appellate Courts have held that other activities, such as operating heavy equipment, may cause repetitive motion conditions which may be the basis of a workers' compensation claim.

Although there is no statute or case law to support a claim for back injuries as a result of repetitive motions, the author's law firm has successfully handled several cases for workers who collected full workers' compensation benefits as a result of repetitive motion resulting in back injury.

SILICOSIS AND ASBESTOSIS ARE TREATED DIFFERENTLY

The conditions of silicosis and asbestosis are both occupational diseases which are treated differently under North Carolina law.

Silicosis is defined as the characteristic fibrotic condition of the lungs caused by breathing in dust of silica or silicates. Industries in which workers may be exposed to silica dust include brick-making, or any industry in which sand and gravel are handled frequently. Asbestosis is defined as the characteristic fibrotic condition of the lungs caused by the inhalation of asbestos dust. Asbestos was widely used in industry years ago. Although it is no longer in use, many buildings still contain asbestos and workers continue to be exposed. Asbestosis has an extremely long latency period, which means that a worker who is exposed to asbestos 20 or 30 years ago may not yet exhibit the signs and symptoms of asbestosis.

Both silicosis and asbestosis are extremely serious occupational diseases, for which there is no cure, and which eventually completely disable the victim.

The North Carolina General Assembly has enacted special rules which apply only to the victims of silicosis and asbestosis.

They provide that if the worker has been exposed to asbestos or silicosis for as much as 30 working days, or parts thereof, within seven consecutive calendar months, such exposure shall be deemed injurious. This means that the worker does not have to establish that the conditions of his or her employment with the defendant caused or significantly contributed to his disease. In this case, the worker need only show that: 1) he has the occupational disease, and 2) he was last injuriously exposed to the hazards of such disease in the defendant's employment.

When the Industrial Commission is advised by an employer or employee that the employee has asbestosis or silicosis, the Industrial Commission will order the employee to submit to X-rays and a physical examination by a special advisory committee set up by the Industrial Commission.

If the first examination reveals that the worker does have asbestosis or silicosis, the Industrial Commission shall order that the employee be removed from any occupation which exposes him or her to the hazards of asbestosis or silicosis. The worker will also be entitled to collect compensation benefits at the rate of 2/3 of the workers' average weekly wage for a period of 104 weeks. The worker is entitled to at least 104 weeks of benefits even if he remains able to work. This rule was enacted to encourage the employee to change occupations and remove himself from harmful exposure. It is unnecessary to show disability in order to receive the initial 104 weeks of compensation if asbestosis or silicosis is diagnosed.

After the first examination, the employee must submit himself to a second and third examination to determine if there is disability resulting from the exposure to asbestos or silicon.

If the employee becomes totally disabled, he or she will be entitled to lifetime benefits.

If the incapacity to work is only partial, the employer shall pay to the employee 2/3 of the difference between the pre-disability income and the income earned after the partial disability. These benefits will only be paid, however, for an additional 196 weeks after the initial 104 weeks of full workers' compensation benefits.

Should death result from the asbestosis or silicosis within 350 weeks from the date of the last exposure and while the employee is entitled to compensation for disablement, either partial or total, the family of the deceased worker would be entitled to full death benefits as discussed in section 13.

If the worker has asbestosis or silicosis and dies from any other cause, the family of the deceased worker will be entitled to certain benefits as a result of having contracted the asbestosis or silicosis.

If tuberculosis develops and complicates disability due to silicosis and/or asbestosis, compensation will be reduced by 1/6.

Claims resulting from exposure to asbestos and silicon are complex. An experienced workers' compensation attorney should be consulted if you feel you have a claim arising from such exposure.

WHERE DISEASE RESULTS FROM AN ACCIDENT

The previous section of this book deals with occupational disease in which diseases occur as a result of work conditions. In those cases, occupational diseases are compensable and the victims of those diseases can recover workers' compensation payments.

This section deals, however, not with occupational diseases, but with diseases which result directly from an accident. While these diseases are unusual, they do occur with sufficient frequency to warrant discussion here.

Diseases which are not inherent in, or incident to, the nature of the employment, but which result from an accident arising out of and in the course of employment are fully compensable. One example is a case of a man who had been in good health up to the time he fell from a platform and broke his leg. After the fall, he lay where he fell for an hour and a half during which time he was exposed to cool weather. After he was discovered, he was taken to the office where he waited two hours for medical attention. The man developed an acute kidney infection which resulted in his death. The court determined that this evidence was sufficient to support an award of full compensation benefits for his death. This is true even though the broken leg, by itself, would not have killed him.

When a worker injured his eye and later contracted a serious eye infection, the court held that the infection was related to the accident which injured the eye and was therefore payable.

Another worker injured in a fall developed myelitis, an inflammatory disease of the spinal cord which can cause fever, muscle stiffness, pain, weakness, and even paralysis. The court held that the employer was liable for the myelitis.

Ordinarily, heart disease is not an injury and is not payable under the workers' compensation law. However, where a policeman suffered a fatal heart attack some ten months after subduing a violent person who resisted arrest and was required to carry the person up three flights of stairs, the court ruled that the policeman's death resulted not from inherent weakness or disease of the heart, but from an unusual and unexpected happening, and that therefore the death resulted from an accident and was payable.

On the other hand, in another case, the court denied recovery for a worker who suffered a coronary occlusion while rolling a heavy rope net in the course of his employment. In that case, a medical doctor testified that the exercise could not be the cause of the condition, although the coronary occlusion might have been accelerated or precipitated by the exertion.

When a worker was struck in the back of the head while at work and later developed an infection in his brain which caused total disability, the court upheld a ruling by the Industrial Commission that his death was caused by an accident arising out of and in the course and scope of his employment.

Benefits were denied for the death of a worker who died from pneumonia. The evidence in that case was that the employee got wet washing machines, and thereafter went outside and worked in the sunshine and open air. The sudden change in temperature caused him to contract pneumonia from which he died.

These cases indicate again how inconsistently the court rules on these cases and how difficult it is to predict whether workers' compensation benefits will be payable. This underscores the need for a good, experienced workers' compensation attorney to help the worker win these cases.

SECTION 15
HOW DO YOU MAKE A CLAIM?

THE ACCIDENT MUST BE REPORTED IN WRITING QUICKLY

The law requires that the injured employee or his representative immediately, on the occurrence of an accident, or as soon thereafter as possible or at least within 30 days, give a written notice of the accident to the employer.

Don't panic if this written notice has not been given. Actually, it is very rare for an employee to give actual written notice to the employer. In most cases the employee gives a verbal report of the accident to his or her supervisor. It is the supervisor or someone else in management who makes a written report. If written notice is given at all, it is usually after an attorney is retained. After an attorney is hired, the attorney sends written notice.

The written notice does not need to be complicated. All that is required is that the notice state in ordinary language the name and address of the employee; the time, place, nature and cause of the accident; and of the resulting injury or death. Notice shall be signed by the employee or someone on his behalf. The following is an example of a notice which will meet the requirements of the statute:

To Progress Energy, my employer:
I was injured while working at my job on January 10,
2006 at approximately 10:00 a.m. when I lost my balance and
fell from a ladder at the 200 Industrial Drive Plant. When I
fell to the concrete floor, I injured my back. Joe Smith,
employee, 150 Oak Street, Raleigh, North Carolina.

With respect to occupational diseases other than asbestosis, silicosis, or lead poisoning, the time requirement for notice to the employer of the occupational disease is the same as set out above and runs from the date that the employee has been advised by a competent medical authority that he has the occupational disease as well as the nature and work related cause of the disease.

The occupational diseases of asbestosis, silicosis, and lead poisoning involve a separate set of complex rules and regulations. Any employee who suspects he may have any of these conditions should immediately contact an experienced workers' compensation attorney.

Most hearing officers will not deny a claim based upon failure to give written notice within 30 days. This is especially true if the employer had actual notice of the accident and cannot show that the employer's failure to receive written notice put the employer at a disadvantage.

It is rare that a factual situation would result in a finding that the employer was so prejudiced or damaged by the failure of the employee to give written notice within 30 days that the claim would be denied. However, it has happened.

CLAIMS MUST BE FILED WITH THE
N.C. INDUSTRIAL COMMISSION
WITHIN TWO YEARS

Although great latitude is given to the injured worker for failure to file a written notice of accident with the employer, no such latitude is given with respect to the requirement that the claim be filed with the N.C. Industrial Commission within two years of the date of the accident.

North Carolina statutes provide that: "The right to compensation shall be... forever barred unless a written claim is filed with the Industrial Commission within two years after the date of the accident."

This claim is filed on a form called a "Form 18" which is provided by the Industrial Commission. If this Form 18 is properly filled out and submitted to the Industrial Commission within two years of the date of the accident, the filing requirement is satisfied and the claim may proceed. However, if such written notice is not submitted to the Industrial Commission within the appropriate time, the claim is forever barred and there can be no recovery.

The time requirement for filing a written claim with the Industrial Commission is rigid. Even where all parties consent to a late filing, such consent is not sufficient to overcome the bar which prevents any further action.

It does not cost anything to file this claim with the Industrial Commission, and there is no reason not to file it just as soon as the accident occurs.

With respect to occupational diseases, (other than asbestosis, silicosis or lead poisoning) a claim must be filed with the

Industrial Commission within two years after the employee's death, disability, or disablement, as the case may be a result of such occupational diseases. The worker is not considered "disabled" until he becomes unable to earn the wages he was earning at the time of the incapacity. The rule is somewhat different with respect to an occupational disease caused by exposure to radiation.

These rules with respect to filing a claim may be subject to certain very narrow exceptions. However, the safest course of conduct, and the one that should be followed in every case, is to file a written claim with the North Carolina Industrial Commission as soon as possible.

It is important in preparing the Form 18 to list all of the injuries that are suspected to have occurred in connection with the work related injury or occupational disease. When in doubt, be as inclusive as possible. Failure to list any body part or organ in the Form 18 could result in a denial of a claim based upon that omitted body part or organ. For instance, if a worker feels that the primary injury was a broken arm, but he also injured his knee, which gives him fewer problems, the worker should list both the arm and the knee on the Form 18, even if he does not feel the knee will give him significant problems in the future.

The best procedure for filing a notice of the injury or occupational disease with the employer and for filing the claim with the Industrial Commission is to use Form 18 which must be filed with the Industrial Commission in any event. By sending a copy of the Form 18 to the employer, the notice requirement to the employer is thereby satisfied. However, the notice to the employer must be delivered to the employer within 30 days of the accident or occupational disease. Although the law allows up to two years within which to file a notice of claim with the North Carolina Industrial Commission, there is no reason to wait.

An example of a properly completed Form 18 is found in the Appendix to this book.

SECTION 16
DISABILITIES

WHAT IS A DISABILITY?

"Disability," as defined in North Carolina workers' compensation law, means "incapacity, because of injury, to earn the wages which the employee was receiving at the time of the injury at the same or any other employment."

Disability is related to wage loss and not to physical infirmity. Disability is the event of being incapacitated for the performance of normal labor. Disability is more than a mere physical injury.

A finding of disability is a requirement for an award of compensation unless the injured worker chooses to accept benefits under the schedule of injuries referred to in section 13. Unless there is loss of earning capacity, there is no disability within the meaning of the workers' compensation law.

In the workers' compensation setting, there are four kinds of disability:

- Temporary total disability.
- Permanent and total disability.
- Temporary partial disability
- Permanent partial disability.

For temporary total disability, the worker will receive two-thirds of his average weekly wage during the time he is unable to earn any income as a result of the injury or occupational disease arising out of his employment. If the disability is "permanent and total," the worker will receive two-thirds of his average weekly wage for the rest of his life. A worker is entitled to benefits for "temporary partial" disability on the basis of the difference between the average weekly wage he earned prior to becoming disabled and the average weekly wages earned after the injury. The extent of this loss is considered "partial" impairment because the worker can earn some amount of wages, but not as much as he or she earned before the injury or occupational disease. That is, his earning capacity is only partially reduced. The "temporary" aspect of this type of disability arises from the fact that he will recover when the condition improves, and as a result, his earning capacity will be restored in full. He would then no longer be entitled to workers' compensation benefits for this "temporary partial" disability.

The worker who suffers "permanent partial" disability must elect between the following two benefits:

(1) He or she may receive 2/3 of the difference between the average weekly wage earned just before the disability and the wages earned after his return to work. This benefit for permanent partial disability, however, continues only for 300 weeks from the day of injury. After the 300 weeks, the benefits stop. That is one reason employers try to get employees back to any kind of work, regardless of the wages earned because they know that after 300 weeks from the date of the injury, their liability to this worker for compensation benefits other than medical benefits will end. The worker, on the other hand, should resist returning to "any employment"

if such employment is not "suitable" based upon his education, training and experience. The Industrial Commission will not necessarily force a previously high wage earner into a minimum wage type job if it finds that such minimum wage type work is not "suitable." As is discussed elsewhere in this book, the issue of whether a worker can return to work and what is a "suitable employment," is a major battleground fought between employees and employers. It is most important for the injured worker to have the benefit of an experienced workers' compensation lawyer at this stage of the proceedings. See rule 11 in section P.

(2) The worker who suffers a permanent partial disability may elect to receive benefits under the schedule of injuries referred to in section 13 of this book. The worker does not need to prove a loss of wage earning ability in order to receive benefits under the "schedule of injuries" provision. See section 13 No. 1.

The worker cannot recover both benefits. The election as to which benefit to choose should not be made without the guidance of an experienced workers' compensation lawyer. The decision should be made on a case by case basis, taking a multitude of factors into account. An experienced lawyer is best suited to help the worker make those decisions.

PRE-EXISTING CONDITIONS

A worker can recover full workers' compensation benefits when an accident materially accelerates or aggravates a condition which existed before the accident. This is true even if the accident would not have caused injury or death to a person without such a pre-existing condition.

The application of this rule of law arises most often in cases involving injury to the back. The fact that an employee has an injured or weak back before the accident does not prevent the worker from collecting full workers' compensation benefits when an accident at work causes injury to an already injured back. The employment need not be the only cause of injury in order to render the accident payable.

The relative contributions of the accident and the pre-existing condition are not weighed. An employer must accept an employee as he is, and if a compensable injury precipitates a latent physical condition such as heart disease, cancer, back weakness, or the like, the entire disability is payable.

When an injury, arising out of and in the course of the employment, aggravated a pre-existing heart condition and caused death, the court held that the injury was payable.

This rule of law is a great benefit to the injured worker; however, the rule is not always easy to apply. It is sometimes difficult to predict whether the Industrial Commission or the court will determine that an accident caused an injury. Even where there is a claim that an accident made a pre-existing condition worse, the worker still must prove that the accident had some part in causing the injury.

As with many issues arising in workers' compensation cases, the issue of whether an accident or condition at work which makes a pre-existing condition worse is compensable is sometimes difficult to predict. Therefore, it is important to have the assistance of an experienced workers' compensation lawyer to increase the chances of collecting from the employer.

PROVING DISABILITY

The burden of proving that the worker is disabled is upon the worker himself. The injured worker must show by the greater weight of the evidence that he has suffered a loss of earning capacity due to a compensable injury.

In order to support a conclusion of disability, the Industrial Commission must find that the following facts exist:

1. That the injured worker was incapable, after his or her injury of earning the same wage as he or she earned before his or her injury in the same employment.

2. That the injured worker was incapable after his or her injury of earning the same wages he or she earned before the injury in any other employment.

3. That the injured worker's incapacity to earn was caused by his injury at work which arose out of and in the course and scope of his or her employment.

An injured worker may meet this burden of proof in one of the following ways:

1. The introduction of medical evidence that the worker is physically or mentally, as a consequence of the work related injury, incapable of work in any employment.

2. The introduction of evidence that the injured worker is capable of some work, but after a reasonable effort on his part, he has been unsuccessful in his effort to obtain employment.

3. The production of evidence that he is capable of some

work, but that it would be futile because of pre-existing conditions (such as age, inexperience, or lack of education) to seek other employment.

4. The introduction of evidence that the injured worker has obtained other employment at a wage less than that earned before the injury.

SECTION 17
THE EMPLOYER'S DUTY
TO PAY BENEFITS

WHEN ARE WORKERS' COMPENSATION
PAYMENTS DUE?

When an employer admits that the employee is entitled to workers' compensation benefits, the employer is required to begin making weekly workers' compensation payments no later than the 14th day after the employer has written or actual notice of the injury or death. By the 14th day after such notice, the employer shall pay all compensation then due.

Written notice of the claim should be filed with the Industrial Commission on a Form 18. For a sample Form 18, please refer to the Appendix of this book.

After the initial payment which must be made no later than 14 days after notice, the employer is required to make weekly payments.

If any installment of compensation is not paid within 14 days after it becomes due, the worker can collect a penalty in an amount equal to 10 percent of such overdue payment.

◆

If the employer denies the claim, it must notify the employee and the Industrial Commission of this refusal to pay compensation.

After receiving notice of this denial, it is the employee's burden to file a Form 33 with the North Carolina Industrial Commission to ask for a hearing on the issue of whether the employer is obligated to pay workers' compensation benefits to the employee. For a sample Form 33, please refer to the Appendix of this book.

The employer is under no obligation to make workers' compensation payments if it files a denial of the claim. The employer does not have to pay benefits pending a hearing to resolve the issue of its liability to the employee. Interest does not accrue on the employer's liability to pay workers' compensation benefits until the date of the initial hearing.

Once a hearing is conducted on a denied claim, the employer is required to make compensation payments as ordered by the Commission. If the employer fails to make payments as ordered by the Commission within 14 days from the day that each payment is due, the worker is entitled to a 10 percent penalty.

If there is an appeal from the initial hearing to the full Industrial Commission, the employer does not have to make payments to the employee until and unless the full Commission orders such payment.

If the employer denies the worker's claim and the Industrial Commission ultimately finds that the employer is required to pay the employee workers' compensation benefits, the first installment of compensation payable under the terms of an Award by the Industrial Commission shall become due ten days from the day following expiration of the time for appeal from the Award or judgment or the day after notice waiving the right of appeal by all parties has been received by the Industrial Commission, whichever occurs sooner.

The initial determination of the employer's liability to pay workers' compensation benefits if the employer denies the claim is made by a Deputy Industrial Commissioner. A Deputy Industrial Commissioner has the power to rule that the employer is liable to the employee for workers' compensation benefits. The employer may then appeal that decision to the full Industrial Commission. Once the Industrial Commission has ruled, the employer may then appeal to the North Carolina Court of Appeals, a process which usually takes a year and a half to complete.

The provision of the law mentioned above which allows the employer to defer payment of workers' compensation benefits by successive appeals which could last several years places the employee at a huge disadvantage.

This ability to defer payments gives the employer a tremendous bargaining advantage over an employee who is out of a job, and has no income and whose family is dependent upon him or her for basic survival needs.

There is no real deterrent to discourage an employer from using successive appeals to string out the employee. During the appeals process, the employee is left to fend for himself even when he is unemployed, destitute, and has no source of income.

The only adverse consequence to the employer for conducting these successive appeals is his attorneys' fees and other related costs of the appeal. In certain severe cases, the employer may be ordered to pay a portion of the employee's attorney fees. The employer will have to pay interest to the employee from the date of the initial hearing at the legal rate of 8 percent. However, this is no real deterrent since the employer and his insurance carrier is able to hold this money during these appeals and presumably collect interest on the money which is due the employee.

THERE IS A PENALTY FOR LATE PAYMENT

North Carolina law requires prompt payment of workers' compensation benefits. If any installment of compensation is not paid within 14 days after it becomes due there shall be added to such unpaid installment an amount equal to 10 percent which shall be paid at the same time as, but in addition to, the regular workers' compensation payment.

One of the most frequent reports we receive regularly in our office is that the workers' compensation insurance company is late in making weekly workers' compensation payments.

Injured workers and their families depend upon these weekly workers' compensation payments to help replace the wages that have been lost by the injured worker's inability to return to work. If these payments are late, it puts the worker and his family in financial distress. There is not much that can be done for the worker, however, until the payment is 14 days late. After that time, a 10 percent penalty can be collected.

In extreme cases, where the insurance carrier fails to make any payment at all, the worker can ask that the Industrial Commission hold the employer in contempt of the orders of the North Carolina Industrial Commission. The contempt powers of the Industrial Commission are a very effective tool to enforce payments.

In order to avoid a 10 percent penalty for being more than 14 days late in making workers' compensation payments, the employer would have to show that the failure to pay was due to conditions over which he had no control. The Industrial Commission rarely excuses the employer from paying the 10 percent penalty for late payments.

INTEREST ON WORKERS' COMPENSATION BENEFITS.

Once there is an Order issued either granting or denying workers' compensation benefits and there is an appeal resulting in an ultimate award to the employee, the employer shall pay interest on the final Award from the date of the initial hearing on the claim until paid. The rate of interest due is 8 percent. This provision of the law was enacted to prevent employers from delaying payment of workers' compensation awards by use of a frivolous appeal. Under this law interest runs at 8 percent not from the final decision on the appeal, but from the date of the initial hearing. Notice that interest is due from the date of the initial hearing, even if the employee lost in the initial hearing and appealed from that loss. Interest, of course, will not be paid unless the employee ultimately prevails on this claim and is awarded workers' compensation benefits.

WORKER GETS TEN PERCENT INCREASE IN BENEFITS IF EMPLOYER VIOLATES SAFETY STATUTE

An injured worker is entitled to a ten percent increase in benefits when a worker's injury or death is caused by the willful failure of the employer to comply with any statutory requirement or any lawful order of the Industrial Commission.

While the statute provides that a violation of any statutory requirement which causes the injury or death of the injured worker gives a rise to the 10 percent increase in benefits, the usual application of this statute is with respect to an OSHA violation or the violation of some other safety statute. One example of the application of this statute is a case in which an increase in the employee's compensation award of 10 percent was upheld when the employer had violated OSHA standards by failing to have a guard on a brake press machine and the employee established that the failure to have the guard was the cause of the injury.

SECTION 18
EMPLOYER DEFENSES

VIOLATION OF SAFETY STANDARD
BY EMPLOYEE

Workers' compensation benefits will be reduced by 10% if an employee violates a safety standard. Under that law when the injury or death is caused by the willful failure of the employee to use a safety appliance or perform a statutory duty or by the willful breach of any rule or regulation adopted by the employer and approved by the commission and brought to the knowledge of the employee prior to the injury, compensation would be reduced by 10 percent. This is a narrow exception to the general rule that the negligence on the part of an employee which causes injury or death will not prevent the payment of workers' compensation benefits. An employee who injured himself when a crane he was improperly operating toppled over was not prevented from collecting workers' compensation benefits because there was no evidence that his injuries were the result of a willful intention to injure himself or a willful breach of a safety rule or procedure adopted by his employer. Although the worker was clearly negligent and his negligence caused his injury, the worker still recovered.

INJURED EMPLOYEE CANNOT RECOVER IF HIS INJURY OR DEATH WAS CAUSED BY HIS INTOXICATION OR BY HIS BEING UNDER THE INFLUENCE OF CONTROLLED SUBSTANCES.

If an injured worker is intoxicated or under the influence of controlled substances and if that intoxication or influence of controlled substances caused the injury, there can be no recovery for the injured or killed worker. This does not mean that the worker who was intoxicated cannot recover for a workers' compensation claim. It is only when the employer can prove that the intoxication caused the injury that the employer can avoid paying the worker's claim. The issue of whether a worker's intoxication was the cause of the injury is a fact issue to be decided by the North Carolina Industrial Commission. One illustrative case involved an employee who was injured when his blood alcohol level was .387 soon after the accident. The Industrial Commission found that the employee's intoxication was not the proximate cause of his injury sustained when his hand got stuck on a lumber conveyer. In another case the Industrial Commission found that the claimant's intoxication was not a proximate cause of an accident even though the claimant's blood alcohol level was .11 to .13 at the time of the accident. In that case the worker had a preexisting mental and visual handicap and the equipment provided by his employer malfunctioned. His supervisor testified he did not smell alcohol on the claimant's breath and that he felt perfectly safe in having the claimant operating the equipment.

THE WORKER INTENTIONALLY
INJURES HIMSELF

An injured worker will not be able to collect workers' compensation benefits if his employer can prove that the employee intentionally injured himself. The employer must show that the injured worker had the willful intention to injure himself and that this intention was the cause of the claimant's injuries.

It is not necessary for the employer to show that the injured worker intended to inflict "serious injury" upon himself. If the employer can show that the employee only intended to inflict minor injuries, but that, the employee suffered unintentional serious injuries, the worker's claim will be denied.

SECTION 19
WHAT IF THE EMPLOYER DENIES THE INJURED WORKER'S CLAIM FOR COMPENSATION BENEFITS?

If the employer and the injured employee or his dependents fail to reach an agreement regarding an application for workers' compensation benefits, or if there is a disagreement concerning any other aspect of the claim, either party may apply to the Industrial Commission for a hearing. This application should be on a Form 33, an example of which can be found in the Appendix of this book.

The Form 33 will be filed with the Industrial Commission, and a copy served upon the opposing party. The opposing party is then required to file a Form 33R whereon the response to the Form 33 request for hearing is made.

After a Form 33 has been filed, the Industrial Commission will set a date for hearing. The Industrial Commission will notify the parties of the time and place for the hearing. The hearing will usually be held in the city or county where the injury occurred.

The injured worker should not attempt to prepare and file a Form 33 on his own, but should instead seek the services of an experienced workers' compensation lawyer.

If the employee and the employer are in disagreement on any issues such that a hearing must be held, the employee should not fight this battle alone. There are many technicalities and variables upon which the outcome of a case could be determined. While there is no specific requirement that an employee be represented by an attorney at a hearing before the N.C. Industrial Commission, an employee would be foolish not to hire an attorney to prepare the Form 33 and to represent him at the hearing.

MEDIATION

Once a Form 33 request for hearing has been filed, the Industrial Commission will order that the case go to mediation.

Mediation is nothing more than a settlement conference presided over by a mediator.

The Industrial Commission gives both parties an opportunity to agree upon a mediator. If the parties cannot agree, a mediator will be appointed by the Industrial Commission. A mediator is usually a lawyer or a retired judge. The mediator is independent and does not take sides with either party. The mediator is like a referee who has no interest in the outcome of the case.

It is the mediator's job to get the parties together and to try to settle the case.

The mediated settlement conference begins with a meeting of all parties and their lawyers with the mediator. The mediator gives each side an opportunity to explain its position in the case. Thereafter, each party goes into separate rooms. The mediator moves back and forth between the rooms carrying demands and offers between the parties and tries to bring the parties closer to settlement with each trip. The ultimate goal is for the parties to reach an agreement and settle the case.

One advantage of using a mediator to settle the case is that each party can tell the mediator the amount for which they would be willing to settle. The mediator does not divulge this number to the other side without permission. Therefore, the mediator, and only the mediator, will know the final position of each side and will, therefore, be in a better position to bring the parties together.

The Industrial Commission orders mediation in every case. A case cannot be heard by a Deputy Industrial Commissioner before mediation.

The mediation process has worked surprisingly well, and it is estimated that well over half of the cases are settled in mediation. This is a great benefit to the injured worker because his case is settled quickly and in an amount that satisfies the worker's demand.

HEARING BEFORE THE DEPUTY INDUSTRIAL COMMISSION

The Industrial Commission will usually assign a deputy industrial commissioner to hear the case. A hearing before the deputy industrial commissioner is much like a trial in civil court except that there is no jury. The deputy industrial commissioner sits as a judge and also decides the factual issues in question.

The law requires the deputy commissioner to decide the case within 180 days of the close of the hearing unless it extends time for good cause.

APPEAL TO THE FULL INDUSTRIAL COMMISSION

If either party is dissatisfied with the ruling of the deputy commissioner, the party may file an appeal to the full

Industrial Commission which shall review the award. The case will then be decided, not by deputies, but by a panel of three Industrial Commissioners. New evidence is usually not presented at the appeal hearing to the full Industrial Commission. The full Industrial Commission has the authority to issue a completely new decision and make new findings of fact and may make findings of fact contrary to the facts found by the deputy commissioner.

APPEAL TO THE APPEALATE COURTS

An appeal from the full Industrial Commission can be made to the North Carolina Court of Appeals, the second highest court in the state. However, for this appeal, only issues of law would be decided. The Court of Appeals will uphold any factual issue decided by the Industrial Commission if there is any evidence to support that finding. In rare cases, there may be an appeal to the Supreme Court of North Carolina.

SECTION 20
TERMINATION OF BENEFITS

Once the right to workers' compensation payments has been established, the employer may not terminate these benefits without specific approval by order of the North Carolina Industrial Commission. An exception to this rule is when the employee returns to work.

Unless the injured employee returns to work, the employer who wishes to stop payment of workers' compensation benefits must petition the Industrial Commission for approval. This petition must be on a form prescribed by the Industrial Commission and a copy must be given to the employee and the employee's attorney. This form shall contain the reasons for the proposed termination or suspension of compensation. It must be supported by available documentation and it must inform the employee of the employee's rights to contest the termination or suspension by filing an objection in writing with the Industrial Commission within 14 days of the date the employer's notice is filed with the Industrial Commission. If the employee fails to object to the petition to terminate benefits within the time provided, the Industrial Commission may, and most probably will, terminate or suspend the compensation to the employee.

If the employee files a timely objection to the petition to terminate benefits, the Industrial Commission shall conduct an informal hearing by telephone with the parties or their lawyers. If either party objects to conducting the hearing by telephone, the Industrial Commission may, but is not required to, conduct the hearing in person in Raleigh or at another location selected by the Industrial Commission.

At this informal hearing, the parties are given an opportunity to state their position and to submit documentary evidence.

The hearing must be conducted within 25 days of the receipt by the Industrial Commission of the employer's petition to terminate benefits.

The Industrial Commission is required to issue a decision on the employer's application for termination of compensation within five days after the informal hearing. The commission may approve or disapprove of the application or, if it is unable to reach a decision, may schedule a formal hearing before a deputy commissioner of the Industrial Commission.

Only in the event that the employer's application to suspend payments is approved may compensation be stopped. If the commission was unable to reach a decision, the employee's compensation shall continue until a decision is reached by the Industrial Commission after the formal hearing.

If the employer's application to terminate or suspend benefits is allowed after the informal telephone hearing, the employer may, at that point, stop paying workers' compensation payments. Even if there is an appeal from the ruling, the employer does not have to continue making payments pending the appeal.

If the Industrial Commission denies the employer's decision to terminate benefits after the informal telephone hearing, the employer must continue paying workers' compensation payments to the employee. This is true even if there is an appeal and request for a formal hearing.

The Industrial Commission's decision in the informal hearing is not binding on either party and either party may appeal and ask for a formal hearing before a deputy commissioner.

At this hearing after the appeal, a new hearing is conducted from scratch without any factor in the informal hearing decision playing a part in the formal hearing. All evidence is presented anew at the formal hearing.

If after a formal hearing, the employer's request to terminate benefits is allowed, the employer may terminate benefits effective from the date the employer first filed the petition to terminate. At this point the employer will be entitled to a credit for the overpayment which will have accrued during the hearing and appeal process.

Among the most common basis for the employer's petition to terminate benefits are the following:

(1) *The employee is no longer disabled.* The employer will argue that the injured worker's condition has improved to the point at which he is able to return to work full-time at his previous job or at some other job.

The employer will argue that the worker could find another job if he really tried. This is when the injured workers' job search log is very valuable. If a legitimate job search has been unsuccessful, chances are good that the workers' compensation benefits will not be terminated.

(2) *The injured worker has refused suitable employment.* The issue here becomes whether the worker can actually do the job that the employer has offered him. The treating doctor's testimony is very important on this issue.

As soon as an allegation of refusing suitable employment is made, the injured worker should hire a vocational expert to test and examine the worker and read his medical and vocational as well as other records to form an opinion concerning whether the employment offered to the worker is in fact "suitable."

While medical testimony is always important, the issue involving suitable employment and whether a worker is in fact employable is more within the expertise of a vocational expert. The vocational expert will, of course, rely heavily upon medical records, but this expert will also conduct vocational testing and study the employee's education, vocational skills, government employment statistics, work history and other materials upon which to form an opinion.

(3) *The worker refused to co-operate with vocational rehabilitation efforts or refused to be examined by a doctor chosen by the employer.* The injured worker should never let it be said that he refused to co-operate with vocational rehabilitation efforts or that he ever refused to be examined by a doctor. Resistance to vocational rehabilitation and to examinations by doctors should never be in the form of a flat-out refusal. Such resistance, if conducted at all, should only be after close consultation with an experienced workers' compensation attorney.

Please refer to sections N and P of this book concerning how to deal with vocational rehabilitation counselors and with doctors.

By following the advice in the book, a worker should not have to defend against an effort to terminate his workers' compensation benefits.

If a petition to terminate benefits is filed, the worker should call his lawyer immediately. If he does not have a lawyer at this point, he should retain an experienced workers' compensation lawyer immediately. The issues involved will be too complex for him to handle himself. The amount of money at issue is large enough to justify the expense of a lawyer.

For failure to co-operate with vocational rehabilitation efforts, the Industrial Commission may only "suspend" workers' compensation benefits, not terminate them. When the employee starts cooperating with vocational rehabilitation efforts, his benefits should be resumed.

WHAT SHOULD A WORKER DO WHEN HIS EMPLOYER SAYS THAT HE SHOULD COME BACK TO WORK?

North Carolina law provides that an injured worker's benefits will be terminated if he refuses suitable employment. See discussion of this issue in section 20.

If you are attempting to return to work with various work restrictions (such as a 10 pound weight restriction with no bending, lifting, or stooping), you should be sure that your employer intends to comply with those limitations. While you should report to work as instructed, under no circumstances should you do work which is outside of the limitations established by your treating doctor.

You should keep a photo copy of your doctor's return to work restrictions so that you can show it to any supervisor or boss in the event that he asks you to do work outside those restrictions. If your employer insists that you do work outside your restrictions, tell your employer politely that you would like to do the work but your doctor will not allow you to do the work which is outside your restrictions. You should then call your lawyer at the first opportunity.

The important thing that you should always do is show up for work. This is true even if you suspect that your employer may try to coerce you into working outside your restrictions. You should never give your employer an excuse to terminate your benefits. If you are instructed to return to work, you should do so. This is especially true if the doctor has approved of your returning to this particular job. Failure to return to work will most likely result in the termination of your benefits. You may also be fired by your employer. It is better to show up at the job site, clock in, and do nothing than it is to fail to show up for work.

You should make it clear to your employer that you are willing to do any kind of work so long as such work is not outside of the work restrictions that your doctor placed upon you. Once your benefits are suspended or terminated, it is usually very difficult to have these benefits restored.

The point at which you are required to return to work is a very crucial stage in the progress of your workers' compensation claim. You should not attempt to deal with this matter without the assistance of an experienced workers' compensation lawyer.

TRIAL RETURN TO WORK

One of the most dangerous stages of a workers' compensation claim is when the employer tries to get the injured worker back to work.

The law provides that if an injured employee refuses employment found for him suitable to his capacity, he shall not be entitled to any compensation at any time during the continuance of such refusal unless the Industrial Commission finds that the refusal is justified.

The dilemma for the employee arises from another law which provides that workers' compensation benefits will stop when the employee returns to work.

The risk to the injured employee is that after working several weeks he may find that he is, in fact, still unable to do the work. If he is unable to do the work, his employer could fire him. At this point he is left without a job and without workers' compensation benefits. Once workers' compensation benefits are stopped for any reason, it is extremely hard to get these benefits reinstated. Even when they are reinstated, it may take months or years before a final determination.

This risk is the primary factor behind the reluctance of the injured worker to return to work.

Of course, it is in the best interest of the injured worker to go back to work provided he can do so successfully. It is also in the best interest of the employer and his workers' compensation insurance carrier that the worker returns to work.

To assist the worker in dealing with this dilemma, the North Carolina General Assembly enacted legislation dealing with trial return to work. Under this special statute, a worker may return to work for a trial period not to exceed nine months. During this trial return to work, the worker and his doctor may determine whether he can, in fact, continue to work successfully. If the trial return to work is unsuccessful, the law requires the employer to immediately resume paying full workers' compensation benefits without having a hearing or other proceeding.

To facilitate this law, the North Carolina Industrial Commission established a set of regulations and forms dealing with trial return to work. Under these regulations, when the employee returns to work, the employer must file a form known as Form 28T with the Industrial Commission and provide a copy to the employee. If, during the trial return to work period, the employee must stop working due to an injury for which compensation had been paid, the employee should file with the Industrial Commission a Form 28U. This Form 28U must contain a statement completed by the worker's doctor certifying that the injury for which compensation had been paid prevents the employee from continuing the trial return to work. The regulation provides that upon receipt of this Form 28U from the employee, the employer "shall promptly resume payment of compensation for temporary disability."

This is a good law. It serves the purpose of both the employer and the employee. If the law is obeyed, it relieves the

◆

employee from the concern that he may not be able to successfully return to work and, therefore, suffer a long period of time during which he is both out of work and not receiving workers' compensation benefits. It serves the purpose of the employer because it encourages workers to go back to work. The intended effect of this law is that, upon the worker's properly filing the Form 28U which includes his doctor's signature attesting to the fact that his return to work was unsuccessful, the worker will immediately receive full workers' compensation benefits without the hassle and worry and delay caused by a subsequent hearing.

Although this is a very good law, in practice, the results have been mixed. The problem arises from the fact that employers can simply thumb their nose at the law and dream up every excuse imaginable to support their failure to resume payment of full workers' compensation benefits after an unsuccessful return to work effort. The law does not give the Industrial Commission sufficient teeth to provide a real deterrent to the employers from this kind of misconduct.

In practice, the worker is still at risk when he returns to work. It is important to be absolutely certain that he can successfully do the job on a long-term basis. Otherwise, he runs the risk of a long delay while the issue of payment of further workers' compensation benefits is being decided.

The risk of returning to work, however, should be measured against the real risk of failing to return to work when the employer and doctor say that the employer can return. If the Industrial Commission finds that the worker refused suitable employment offered to him, the worker will not be entitled to any further compensation during the continuance of such refusal.

If the injured worker refuses to return to work, it is important to have a strong doctor's opinion supporting this refusal.

Because the decision to return to work is so full of risks, it is also essential to have an experienced workers' compensation lawyer involved in all aspects of this decision.

DO NOT GIVE THEM AN EXCUSE
TO FIRE YOU WHEN YOU RETURN TO WORK

You should use extreme caution when you return to work after any workers' compensation injury. Be sure not to give your employer any reason to fire you.

It is possible that if you are terminated, the court will construe the conduct which led to the termination to have been a constructive refusal to return to work. In that case, you may not be able to resume collection of workers' compensation benefits even if your injury prevents you from returning to your full duties.

One example is the case of a lady who returned to light duty work and was fired for alleged gross misconduct after she exposed her buttocks to two female co-employees. The Industrial Commission refused to reinstate her workers' compensation payments because it held that, by this misconduct, she constructively refused suitable employment.

If the employer can show that an employee was legitimately terminated and that a non-disabled employee ordinarily would have been terminated for the same conduct, then the employer has created a rebuttable presumption that the employee's misconduct constituted a constructive refusal to perform the work provided. Unless the worker can rebut that presumption, workers' compensation benefits will not be payable.

However, the employee can rebut that presumption by showing that the inability to find or hold other employment is due to a work-related disability.

IT IS IMPORTANT TO REGULARLY CONDUCT A JOB SEARCH

The employee has the burden of proving that he or she is disabled as a result of a work related injury or occupational disease. Disability is defined as the: "incapacity because of injury to earn wages which the employee was receiving at the time of the injury in the same or any other employment." This ongoing burden of proof which has been placed upon the employee continues even if the employer is continuing to pay temporary total disability benefits to the employee. At any time the employer could file a form with the N.C. Industrial Commission which alleges that the employee is able to return to work. At that point, the employee, not the employer, has the burden to prove that he or she is disabled.

That is, the employee must prove that he does not have the capacity, because of the injury, to earn wages which he was receiving at the time of the injury in the same or any other employment. See section 16.

Testimony of the employee's doctor to the effect that the employee cannot work at any job is one way to prove disability. However, in those instances in which the doctor says that the employee can do some work, but that the employee is subject to restrictions on the type of physical work he or she can do, an additional method of proving disability must be used.

This additional method is to show that because of the injury, the employer is unable to find a job which does not impose physical requirements upon the employee in excess of those restrictions set by the doctor. In other words, the employee must show that he was unable to find a job within the restrictions imposed by the doctor.

An example of such restrictions would be in the case of a brick layer who has worked all his life doing jobs which require hard physical labor and has work restrictions from his doctor forbidding him to lift more than 10 pounds. Obviously, this worker cannot continue working as a bricklayer since bricklayers are required to lift heavy weights constantly. The question then becomes, is there any job which this bricklayer can do even though he can not lift more than ten (10) pounds. It will probably be difficult for this bricklayer to find a job which would not require him to lift more than 10 pounds. This is especially true if the worker has a very limited education and is advanced in years.

A secretary on the other hand who has a 10-pound weight restriction would probably be able to find a job since a secretary's job usually does not require lifting as much as 10 pounds. Even if the secretary were injured at a job which required lifting more than 10 pounds, chances are it would be easy for him or her to find a job as a secretary that did not require more than 10 pounds of lifting. It is relatively easy to predict how the Industrial Commission would rule on the issue of whether the bricklayer and the secretary are disabled with a 10-pound weight restriction. The bricklayer most likely would be considered disabled, while the secretary most likely would not be considered disabled. However, with occupations which have physical demands between those of a bricklayer and a secretary, it may be hard to predict whether the Industrial Commission would consider a weight restriction or other physical restrictions to be disabling.

A favorite trick the insurance companies use to defeat an injured worker's claim is to pay temporary total disability for a while without assigning a vocational rehabilitation counselor. The worker is lulled into a false sense of security because the employer continues to pay workers' compensation benefits. Because of this false sense of security, the worker does not look for other work and is therefore not fully prepared to prove disability. The insurance company then files a form with the Industrial Commission asking for a hearing on the issue of whether the employee is disabled. Again, the burden of proof in disability remains with the injured employee.

To protect against this ploy on the part of the insurance company, it is extremely important that the worker conduct a regular and thorough job search. This job search involves checking the want ads in the newspaper, jobs posted with the Employment Security Commission, and even cold calling potential employers to see if work is available within the worker's physical restrictions. This job search is tedious and time-consuming. However, while the job search is going on, the employee continues to receive temporary total disability benefits because he or she is out of work. The injured employee should consider this job search as part of his "regular job." It is not nearly as demanding as full-time work, and it is almost as lucrative.

The employee will be in a much better position to prove disability if he or she can testify about an extensive job search, and show that he made an honest effort to find the work, but that no such work was available.

Fortunately for the worker, the law requires the Industrial Commission to make a determination as to whether a particular worker can find a job. It is not enough for the employer simply to show that jobs are available in the market place. In order for a worker's benefits to be terminated, there must be a finding that this individual worker in question was not able to find employment. With an extensive job search, the worker is in a much better position to keep his benefits from being terminated.

Conducting a job search is not as difficult as it may sound. The appendix to this book contains a sample form for use in this job search. The form should be used for each job application made by the employee. If an application was made in response to a want ad, a copy of the want ad should be taped to the sheet. The sheet should be filled out showing the date the application was made, the person contacted by the employee and whether an in-person interview was conducted. If an in-person interview was conducted, the name of the person conducting the interview and the substance of what was discussed during the interview should be added. If an in-person interview was not conducted, there should be a statement that the proposed employer did not allow for an in-person job interview. The form should contain some description of the job for which application was made and a general description of the employer. Mention should be made of the physical and educational requirements of the job.

If possible, have the person who conducts the job interview sign your job search log to prove that you did attend the interview.

If a worker brings to a termination hearing 20 or 30 of these job search forms and testifies about his efforts to find work, the chances of winning are much greater than if the employee simply testifies that he tried to find a job, but could not find one. If a written record of the job search is not made at the time of each application, it will be difficult for the injured worker to remember the specific facts of the job search. It is much more impressive to bring in written documentation of the job search.

One possible outcome of an extensive job search is that the injured worker may find a good job and return to work at a greater salary than he earned before the injury.

SECTION 21
BEWARE OF REHABILITATION COUNSELORS

If an employer admits liability for the workers' injury or occupational disease, and if he is providing benefits to the injured or disabled worker, the employer is allowed to hire rehabilitation professionals to work with the employee.

The stated purpose for rehabilitation professionals is to promote the medical and vocational rehabilitation of the injured worker.

While this is a worthy goal, and certainly should be the purpose of these rehabilitation professionals, in actual practice, in the vast majority of cases, the real purpose of the rehabilitation professional is vastly different.

It has been the observation of this author, as well as the observation of virtually all lawyers who represent employees in the workers' compensation arena, that the real purpose of the rehabilitation professional is to assist the employer in its effort to terminate the worker's benefits.

The rehabilitation professionals are hired by the insurance companies. The insurance companies dictate each and every aspect of the involvement of the rehabilitation professional and the interaction with the injured worker.

Rehabilitation professionals are, in the vast majority of the cases, employees of large profit-making corporations. In many instances, the rehabilitation professionals are employed as direct full-time employees of a subsidiary of workers' compensation carrier.

The biblical truism that "a man cannot serve two masters" has great application in the field of rehabilitation professionals who work in the workers' compensation arena. These rehabilitation professionals know who pays their salaries and who is responsible for their income and profits. They will not "bite the hand that feeds them."

The N.C. Industrial Commission has promulgated a detailed set of rules for utilization by rehabilitation professionals. Among the requirements set out in these rules is that the rehabilitation professional: "shall exercise independent professional judgment in making and documenting recommendations for medical and vocational rehabilitation for the injured worker, including any alternatives for medical treatment and cost-effective return-to-work options including retraining or retirement. The rehabilitation professional shall realize that the attending physician directs the medical care of an injured worker." This very important requirement of the N.C. Industrial Commission is largely ignored in practice by rehabilitation professionals.

The author personally knows at least one rehabilitation professional who was fired by his employer, a large corporation providing vocational rehabilitation services for insurance companies. This worker was fired because he made honest determinations as to whether workers were disabled, and he refused to bow to demands by the insurance company to say that a worker was not disabled when he honestly felt that the worker was disabled. This employee was fired because he exercised independent judgment in carrying out the duties of his profession. With this type of environment in which vocational rehabilitation professionals work, it is understandable why most of them bow to their employers. In that situation, it takes a strong person to stand up to the insurance companies. If they refuse to do the bidding of their insurance company employers, they do not last long in the profession.

There are a few rehabilitation professionals, however, who do take their work seriously and try their best to do an honest job. It is unfair to these few individuals to paint all rehabilitation professionals with this broad brush. We are therefore careful to point out that there are a few exceptions, but they are in the very small minority.

Rehabilitation professionals fall into two categories which are discussed below:

1. MEDICAL REHABILITATION PROFESSIONALS

The term "medical rehabilitation" refers to the planning and coordination of healthcare services. The rules provide that the goals for medical rehabilitation are: "To assist in the restoration of injured workers as nearly as possible to the worker's pre-injury level of physical function."

These medical rehabilitation professionals are usually registered nurses. The rules dictate that medical case management includes, but is not limited to: "Case assessment, including a personal interview with the injured worker; development, implementation and coordination of a care plan with healthcare providers and with the worker and family; evaluation of treatment results; planning for community re-entry; return to work with employer of injury; and/or referral for further vocational rehabilitation services."

The injured worker's primary contact with a medical rehabilitation professional is at the doctor's office. These medical rehabilitation professionals almost always insist on accompanying the worker on every trip to his doctor's office. As a practical matter, their function is to try to persuade the doctor to employ as little and as inexpensive treatment as possible, and to encourage the doctor to sign forms stating that the employee is able to go back to work and to minimize or eliminate the return to work restrictions set by the doctor.

Towards that end, many of these nurses seek private conferences with the doctor, outside the presence of the employee. During these private conferences, the nurses use all their powers of persuasion to try to convince the doctor that the employee is not injured as seriously as the employee claims, and that the employee is capable of greater physical activity that the employee claims. We hasten to point out again that there are some nurses who exercise their independent judgment and who genuinely are concerned about the welfare of the employee. Hence, although such nurses are in the minority, abuses are not as widespread in the case of medical rehabilitation counselors as exists in the case of vocational rehabilitation counselors. See section O for suggestions on how to deal with medical rehabilitation professionals.

2. *VOCATIONAL REHABILITATION PROFESSIONALS*

When a vocational rehabilitation professional is called into your case, you should have frequent contact with your lawyer. Vocational rehabilitation counselors in the context of workers' compensation activities are in an absolutely corrupt profession. The very few exceptions to this statement are in the small minority. The job of the vocational rehabilitation professional is to terminate your benefits by whatever means are available. You should understand that they are not your friend and that they are working hard against you. Otherwise they would not be able to continue working for insurance companies in the workers' compensation arena. They would simply be eliminated and replaced by someone who will do the biding of the insurance company.

In most of the cases in which the insurance industry seeks to terminate benefits for the employee, that effort will be based upon a report or other work of the vocational rehabilitation professional.

The Industrial Commission will suspend workers' compensation benefits if it finds that the injured employee has not fully cooperated with all vocational rehabilitation efforts. See section P for suggestions on how to deal with the vocational rehabilitation professionals.

SECTION 22
MEDICAL CARE

EMPLOYEE MUST SUBMIT TO MEDICAL EXAMINATION BY DOCTOR CHOSEN BY THE EMPLOYER

The law requires that so long as a person claims workers' compensation benefits, the employee must submit to an examination at reasonable times and places by a duly qualified physician or surgeon designated and paid by the employer or the Industrial Commission. Even if the employer denies the worker's compensation claim and fails to make any payment, so long as the employee makes the claim, he or she must submit to this medical examination.

If the employee refuses to submit to an examination or in any way obstructs the examination requested and paid for by the employer, the workers' right to compensation and his right to take or prosecute any proceeding under the Workers' Compensation Act shall be suspended until such refusal or objection ceases. No compensation shall at any time be payable for the period of obstruction unless, in the opinion of the Industrial Commission, the circumstances justify the refusal or obstruction.

The employee does have the right to have present during the examination any duly qualified physician or surgeon provided and paid for by the employee.

The employee may request that he be relieved of the duty to submit to an examination by the doctor of the employer's choice. However, unless the circumstances are extremely unusual, this request will most probably be denied by the Industrial Commission. It is risky to refuse the request to submit to an examination made by the employer even when the employee files a motion with the Industrial Commission for relief from the requirement that he submit to this examination. The risk to the employee is that even if there is a valid workers' compensation claim, benefits will not be payable during such time as the worker refuses or obstructs the examination.

It is important to note that the employer's right to have the employee examined by a physician of his choice is automatic. This right does not depend upon the employer obtaining an order compelling such examination. All that is required is that the employer "requests" such an examination. Failure to submit to the examination upon the mere "request" by the employer will result in suspension of benefits during the period of time that the refusal continues. Not only does the right to benefits stop during the period of such refusal but the worker is not even allowed to proceed with the claim in the Industrial Commission.

There is a distinction between the employer's request for the employer to "submit himself to examination" and the employer's demand that the employee "accept any medical, hospital or surgical or other treatment or rehabilitative procedure." It is only when such treatment or rehabilitative procedure is first ordered by the Industrial Commission that the employee may lose his rights to benefit upon refusal to submit to the treatment.

The worker should exercise extreme caution when the employer seeks to have the worker change medical providers. When this occurs the worker should consult an experienced workers' compensation attorney to help protect against an effort by the employer to "doctor shop." See costly mistake number twelve in section D.

With respect to the employer's request for an examination (as opposed to treatment) there is very little that can be done to prevent such an examination and, in most cases, the worker should submit to this examination. Refer to section N for advice on how to conduct yourself during this examination.

MAY THE EMPLOYEE REFUSE TO ACCEPT TREATMENT?

The employee may refuse surgery or other treatment only if such refusal is reasonable under the circumstances. If such refusal is not reasonable, workers' compensation benefits could be suspended.

In ruling upon whether the employee's decision not to submit to surgery or other medical procedure is reasonable, the Industrial Commission uses a "reasonable person standard." In this setting, the commission must make findings regarding the claimant's ability to act as a "reasonable person" and weigh medical options and make treatment decisions before denying benefits based upon his refusal of treatment.

The courts have upheld a finding by the Industrial Commission that an employee was not justified in choosing to undergo surgery with her own physician where the employer had already accepted liability orally and in writing and was, therefore, entitled to direct the medical treatment and that she did not have good cause to refuse treatment by the employer's physician.

In another case, the court upheld a ruling by the Industrial Commission that the back surgery recommended by one injured worker's physicians had a high probability of significantly reducing the period of the plaintiff's disability and that such treatment would be sought by a similarly situated reasonable man and, therefore, required the injured worker to undergo that surgery or lose his right to compensation.

The court has held that, where the injury to the worker included brain damage to the extent that he became incapable of cooperating with rehabilitation efforts, the policy of liberality construing the Workers' Compensation Act in favor of that injured worker precluded the denial of benefits based upon his willful refusal of treatment.

The court has also held that the reasonableness of a refusal to accept treatment by an employee is measured by whether a reasonable person who is motivated to improve his health would accept the recommended treatment.

MEDICAL CARE IN AN EMERGENCY

If an employee is in an emergency situation and needs medical care because of the employer's failure to provide medical or other care, a physician other than those provided by the employer may be called to treat the injured employee and the reasonable cost of such service shall be paid by the employer "if ordered by the Industrial Commission."

The law with respect to the employee's choice of physician in an emergency situation is quite similar to the law with respect to non-emergency situations. In either case, the Industrial Commission must approve payment for the doctor.

However, it would obviously be more likely that the Industrial Commission would approve payment for medical care necessitated by an emergency than it would otherwise.

Our courts have held that treatment to an employee could be of an emergency nature even though it extended over a seventeen month period of time.

CAN YOU CHANGE DOCTORS?

When an employer accepts liability for a work related injury or condition, the employer gets the right to direct the medical care. This includes the choosing of doctors, hospitals and other healthcare providers.

However, sometimes workers are dissatisfied with the doctors chosen by the employer. The question therefore often arises as to whether the employee can change doctors at will.

The answer is no.

The injured employee may, however, ask the Industrial Commission for permission to change doctors.

The controlling statute in North Carolina provides that if an employee desires, "an injured employee may select a physician of his own choosing to attend, prescribe, and assume the care in charge of his case, subject to the approval of the Industrial Commission."

The "subject to the approval of the Industrial Commission" is a big hurdle. Unless the Industrial Commission has a very good reason to allow the employee to change physicians, the requested change of doctor is usually denied.

Of course, an employee may always consult and be treated by a doctor of his/her choice. However, the risk of doing so is that the Industrial Commission may not require the employer to pay for this medical care.

If a case is being defended by an aggressive workers' compensation insurance company, it will try to direct employees to physicians who they feel will more likely render opinions favorable to the insurance company.

As mentioned, there are some doctors who, for whatever reason, are totally unsympathetic to the plight of the injured worker and consistently render opinions adverse to the employee. If you end up with one of these doctors you should try hard to change doctors and start treatment by an objective fair-minded doctor.

If the situation with the employer's doctor is bad enough, it may be wise to go to another doctor, even without the approval of the Industrial Commission, so that you can present the opinions of the new doctor to the Industrial Commission to support your claim. It is not necessary that a doctor be approved in order to give testimony to the Industrial Commission. It is necessary, however, for a doctor to be approved by the Industrial Commission before the employer will be required to pay for the services of those doctors. If the employer is not required to pay the doctors fees, it may be possible to recover payment for those fees from a health or hospitalization insurance policy issued either to the employee or the employee's spouse.

Theoretically, there is no limit on the number of physicians the employee may choose. However, it is unlikely that the Industrial Commission will approve and require the employer to pay for multiple doctors chosen at the will of the employee.

It is a safer practice to obtain permission from the Industrial Commission before a new doctor is consulted. The risk is that the Industrial Commission may not approve this doctor and the employee will thereby be stuck with the bills. The law requires that application for approval of a change of physician occur within a reasonable time after procuring the services of the physicians.

In order to support an approval by the Industrial Commission for medical treatment rendered by the employee's own physician there must be a finding based upon competent evidence that the treatment was "required to effect a cure or give relief" or that it has "tended to lessen the time of disability." There must also be a finding that the condition treated is or was caused by, or was otherwise traceable, to a work-related injury or condition.

THERE IS NO PHYSICIAN-PATIENT PRIVILEGE

During any interaction with a doctor or other healthcare provider in connection with a workers' compensation matter, anything you tell the doctor or the healthcare provider can, and usually will, be revealed to your adversary.

This is an exception to the general rule in North Carolina that all communications between a patient and a doctor are privileged and may not, under any circumstances, be revealed to third parties without the expressed consent of the patient.

North Carolina law specifically provides that:

"No fact communicated or otherwise learned by any physician or surgeon or hospital or hospital employee who may have attended or examined the employee, or who may have been present at any examination, shall be privileged in any workers' Compensation case with respect to a claim pending for hearing before the Industrial Commission."

Even though you are entitled to consult privately with your physician (as discussed in section N.) the doctor is free to divulge any information you give in that private consultation to any party.

The practical effect of the absence of physician-patient confidentiality is that you can never tell a physician anything that you would not want your employer or its insurance carrier to know.

YOUR EMPLOYER MAY REQUIRE APPROVAL IN ADVANCE BEFORE YOU RECEIVE MEDICAL TREATMENT

It is wise to obtain advance permission from your employer and its workers' compensation insurance carrier before you are admitted to a hospital or treatment center or before you undergo surgery.

North Carolina law provides that a workers' compensation insurance carrier may require preauthorization for inpatient admission to a hospital, inpatient admission to a treatment center, and inpatient or outpatient surgery.

If you receive these medical services without preauthorization there is a strong likelihood that the employer will not have to pay the bill.

As a practical matter, most doctors and hospitals will not perform medical services until they know they are going to be paid. Therefore, these medical providers will themselves seek and obtain preauthorization before they provide treatment.

The law provides certain guidelines which an insurer must follow when imposing a preauthorization requirement.

Among these rules are:

1. The insurer may require no more then ten days advance notice for the inpatient admission or surgery.

2. The insurer must respond to a request for preauthorization within two business days of the request.

3. If the insurer requires the employee to submit to an independent medical examination, the examination must be completed and the insurer must make its determination on the request for preauthorization within seven days of the date of the request. The insurer shall document its review findings and determination in writing and shall provide a copy of the findings and determination to the employee and the employee's doctor or hospital.

4. The insurer <u>shall</u> authorize the inpatient admission or surgery when it requires the employee to submit to a medical examination and the examining physician concurs with the original recommendation for the inpatient admission or surgery. Even if the doctor chosen by the employer does not recommend inpatient hospitalization or surgery, if the doctor chosen by the employee for a second opinion feels that such hospitalization or surgery is necessary, the insurer is required to authorize payment for that admission or surgery.

An insurer may not impose a preauthorization requirement for medical services when the insurer has not admitted liability for the claim.

If an insurer denies liability for the claim, the employee may obtain medical services from the healthcare providers of his or her choice. If it is later determined that the employer and its insurance carrier is liable for the claim, they will have to pay for medical services even though they did not choose the physician or preauthorize the medical services.

Notwithstanding the rules set out above requiring preauthorization before rendering medical treatment, the Industrial Commission may, upon reasonable grounds at the request of the employee or the doctor, authorize treatment if it determines the treatment was reasonably required to affect a cure or give relief.

EMPLOYEES HAVE A RIGHT TO A SECOND OPINION FROM A DOCTOR OF THEIR CHOICE

In those cases in which there is a question as to the percentage of permanent disability suffered by an injured worker, he is entitled to have another examination by a duly qualified physician or surgeon who is licensed to practice in North Carolina or by a duly qualified physician or surgeon licensed to practice in South Carolina, Georgia, Virginia and Tennessee.

The cost of this second opinion shall be born by the employer except for travel expenses.

This right to a second opinion arises only after the claimant has been examined by a physician or a surgeon designated by the employer.

The issue of whether a second opinion should be requested by the employee is very case specific. There is no one answer which fits all circumstances.

The risk of the second opinion is that the second opinion doctor could come in with a lower permanency rating than the rating given by the doctor chosen by the employer.

As discussed in section 19, where there is a dispute as to the degree of permanency suffered by the injured worker, that issue is decided by the Industrial Commission after a hearing.

The permanent disability rating is important because the amount recovered by the injured worker for permanent disability is directly related to the rating. Of course, a higher rating yields a greater recovery for the injured worker than a lower rating.

MEDICAL PROVIDERS CANNOT DEMAND PAYMENT OF HEALTHCARE CHARGES FROM THE EMPLOYEE

North Carolina law makes it a crime for a doctor, hospital, or other health care provider to collect or attempt to collect charges for health care provided to a workers' compensation claimant until such charges have been approved by the Industrial Commission or the court.

Any person who receives any fee, other consideration, or any gratuity for services rendered which have not been approved by the Industrial Commission is guilty of a misdemeanor.

If the injured worker's claim is found to be compensable, the employer will be required to pay all approved fees. The doctor or hospital or other health care provider may not collect any portion of a fee which has not been approved by the Industrial Commission. They may not collect either from the employer or its insurance company or from the employee directly. Therefore, in every case in which the injured employee is entitled to recover medical expenses from the employer, a doctor or hospital or other health care provider may not charge the employee directly.

Even when the employer denies liability for a workers' compensation claim, a doctor, hospital or other health care provider may not pursue a private claim against the employee for all or part of the cost of medical treatment while the workers' compensation claim is pending. No claim may be made against the employee for medical care unless the employee's claim or the treatment is finally adjudicated not to be payable. In other words, a doctor may not pursue payment for medical services from the employee until the claim is finally concluded against the employee. This prohibition against pursuing a private action against the employee continues for as long as the case is pending, even after an initial ruling while the case is on appeal. However, once the case is finally over, if the employee loses, the doctor may then pursue a private claim against the employee for medical services.

If you receive a bill from a doctor for medical services while your workers' compensation claim is pending you should have your lawyer write to the doctor immediately to notify the doctor that his efforts to collect medical bills is a crime and that unless such effort stops immediately, you will pursue your rights against the doctor. The doctor or other health care provider should be cautioned against filing any reports with any credit reporting agencies which would reflect adversely upon your credit.

BE CERTAIN THAT YOU CAN COLLECT FOR FUTURE MEDICAL BENEFITS

Because of the previously unlimited duration of workers' compensation health benefits, big business, industry, and other special interest groups went to the General Assembly in the early 1990s and got a special bill passed which limits the right to continued medical benefits unless the employee takes certain steps to protect himself. Even with this special interest legislation however, the worker can obtain medical benefits which are unlimited in time provided certain precautions are taken. The need and necessity for these special precautions make it important that the injured worker consult with an experienced workers' compensation lawyer.

This special interest legislation provides that: "the right to medical compensation shall terminate two years after the employer's last payment of medical or indemnity (two-thirds of the worker's average weekly wage) compensation unless, prior to the expiration of this period, either (i.) The employee files with the Commission an application for additional medical compensation which is thereafter approved by the Commission, or (ii.) The Commission on its own motion orders additional medical compensation."

It is therefore important, before the two-year expiration date set out above for the worker to ask the Commission for a special order approving additional medical compensation. It is important how this order is drafted. It should be drafted so as to remove any further time limitations.

The worker should not leave it up to the Industrial Commission to enter such an order on its own. The worker must be responsible for looking after himself or herself; therefore the worker must make this motion himself. Be sure that this motion is made before two years has expired from the last payment of medical or weekly workers' compensation benefits. If this motion is not made within that time, the right to future medical benefits is terminated.

The law requires that the Industrial Commission "shall" provide by order for additional payment of "necessary medical compensation" if the Commission determines that there is a substantial risk of the necessity of future medical compensation.

If the injured worker feels that he will continue to need medical benefits beyond two years from the date of the last payment by the employee's medical or indemnity compensation, it is highly advisable that the worker contact a competent experienced workers' compensation attorney. This is true even if the employer and its insurance carrier has been totally fair to the worker up to that point. If, for instance, a doctor advises the worker that he will need surgery at some indeterminate time in the future, it is absolutely necessary that the worker take steps to protect himself to be sure that the employer will be required to pay for such surgery when it is needed. Otherwise, the right to these future medical benefits may be lost. It will not be offered to the worker automatically.

SECTION 23
YOU CAN RECOVER MORE BENEFITS IF YOUR CONDITION WORSENS

If your condition changes and becomes worse after an order or settlement awarding benefits is made, you can apply to the Industrial Commission for additional benefits.

The provision of the law allowing for an increase in benefits does not apply until there has been a previous award of benefits. If there has been no previous award the Industrial Commission will set an appropriate amount of the award at the time of a hearing or settlement. Once this initial hearing or settlement has been made the Industrial Commission may increase that award if there has been a "substantial" change in circumstances.

The courts have construed substantial change as a change in physical capacity to earn wages different from that existing when the previous award was made. A change in physical capacity to earn wages alone is sufficient to support an award of additional compensation for a change of condition. The primary factor in determining whether a change of condition has occurred is whether the employee's physical or mental capacity to earn wages has been affected. A change in the claimants earning capacity even though the claimant's physical condition remains unchanged would justify an increase in benefits.

A change of condition means an actual change and not a mere change of opinion with respect to the existing condition. If, however, the physician examines the claimant subsequent to the date of his first opinion and in the meantime the claimant's physical condition has become worse, then a change of opinion with respect to the degree of permanent partial disability is evidence of a change of condition such as to justify an increase in benefits.

There is a time limit, however, on the ability to go back to the Industrial Commission and ask for increased benefits based upon a changed of circumstances.

The motion for an increase of benefits based upon a change of condition must be made within two years of the date the last compensation payment was made. In a case in which only medical or other healthcare benefits are paid, the motion to increase must be made within 12 months after the last payment of bills for these medical services.

SECTION 24
FINAL SETTLEMENTS

If a worker obtains full workers' compensation benefits for his total impairment he or she will receive his "comp amount" each week for the rest of his life or until he returns to work. The worker cannot require the employer to make payments in advance.

The amount of compensation to which the injured worker is entitled does not change. It stays constant and is not adjusted for inflation or cost-of-living increases. In the case of total and permanent disability, it sometimes is advantageous to both parties to reach an agreement which satisfies the employer's liability to the injured worker in one lump-sum payment. After this one lump-sum payment is satisfied, the employer would then have absolutely no further responsibility for the worker.

These agreements are commonly referred to as "clincher agreements" and lawyers refer to the act of reaching such a settlement as "clinchering" a case.

It costs a lot of money for insurance companies to administer payments to a worker for the rest of his life. The insurance company has to hire staff and maintain computers, office space, and all of the other expenses related to maintaining claimant's files. Even though the amount of weekly benefits is fixed and will not increase in the absence of a change in law, it is not easy to predict the amount the insurance company will have to spend into the future on medical expenses. This is especially true with respect to back injuries which may require multiple surgical procedures. This uncertainty, coupled with the drastic increases experienced in recent years in medical costs makes these long-term workers' compensation claims difficult for the insurance company to evaluate. Insurance companies like to deal in certainties. For a multitude of reasons it sometimes makes sense to an insurance company to try to clincher a long-term workers' compensation claim.

From the standpoint of the injured worker, such a clincher agreement also sometimes makes sense.

If a worker is receiving Social Security disability insurance benefits there is likely an offset or reduction of Social Security benefits because the claimant is receiving worker's compensation benefits. Assuming that the clincher documents are drafted properly, once the clincher agreement is made, the Social Security offset no longer applies and the workers' Social Security disability insurance benefit will increase after weekly workers' compensation benefits stop.

There is a benefit to the employee of not having to deal with all of the complexities of the workers' compensation claim. Having to deal on a regular basis with insurance adjusters is taxing emotionally and it takes a lot of time.

The knowledge that a private detective could be following the claimant around and that at any time the workers' compensation carrier could petition to have the benefits stopped is nerve racking and unsettling to the worker.

A clincher agreement gives some certainty to the worker as well as to the insurance company. It is a great benefit to receive a lump sum of money that is yours no matter what the insurance company does after that point. Workers are concerned that if they were to die suddenly from unrelated causes their workers' compensation benefits would stop and their family would suffer a significant loss of income.

Receiving a large sum of money which will be in the bank for the benefit of the family even if the worker dies, gives the worker piece of mind.

Therefore, provided the payment for the settlement agreement is high enough, it sometimes makes sense for the worker to enter into a clincher agreement.

The injured worker should never try to negotiate a clincher agreement without the assistance of an experienced workers' compensation attorney. It is at this clincher agreement level that the knowledge, experience and expertise of the lawyer really come into play. This is where the lawyer really earns his or her fee. Total and permanent disability workers' compensation claims are very difficult to evaluate, and an experienced workers' compensation lawyer knows how to evaluate these cases and how to draft them properly for the greatest benefit to the injured worker.

Most clincher agreements provide for a lump-sum one-time payment to the injured worker. In exchange for this payment, the worker agrees to give up all claims, past, present, and future against the employer and the insurance company. On rare occasions the insurance company may agree to pay a lump sum to the worker and to pay all related medical expenses into the future as they accrue.

Sometimes the clincher agreement provides for a smaller sum of money to be paid up front and the balance of the clincher obligation to be paid under a structured settlement whereby payments are made to the worker on a periodic basis over a period of years or for the rest of the worker's life. This author advises against such structured settlements. The present workers' compensation law itself is in effect a structured settlement in that it calls for periodic payments to be made on a weekly basis. We see no advantage to the injured worker in these structured settlement arrangements.

As with all settlements, whether they are advantageous for the injured worker depends upon how much the insurance company is willing to pay. Many times the parties do not reach a clincher agreement. Receiving a sum each week equal to two-thirds of their pre-injury gross income which is tax free is not a bad deal for the injured worker. The worker should be paid a large sum to give up this benefit and unless the insurance company is willing to pay a large sum the worker should refuse to settle.

These clincher agreements must be in writing in a form known as a "Memorandum of Agreement" and must be approved by the Industrial Commission. This is true even when the claimant is represented by a lawyer. Before the Industrial Commission will approve this agreement, it will examine each case very carefully, look at all the medical and vocational records, make an independent determination as to whether the agreement is fair and just, and as certain that the interests of all the parties have been considered.

Again, decisions on issues relating to a clincher agreement should never be made without the benefit of an experienced workers' compensation lawyer.

OUR SERVICES

At Brent Adams and Associates we pride ourselves on personal service.

If your case meets our criteria for acceptance, you can be assured that you will receive close, personal attention from our lawyers and our staff. We will keep you advised as to all aspects and stages of your case and keep you fully informed of all developments.

You can call on us at any time should you have any questions about your case or if we can help in any other way.

When you finish your treatment and your case is ready to be resolved, we will carefully advise you as to whether your case should be settled or whether we should take your case to hearing. If we do have a hearing in your case, we will consult with you at every stage of the case and we will decide together what witnesses would be best to call at the hearing.

Our initial consultation with you is absolutely free. After the consultation, there is absolutely no obligation to hire us. If we decide together that we will represent you in your case, we will do so on a contingency fee basis. That means that if we are unable to recover any money for you, we will not charge you a fee. If you choose, we will represent you on an hourly basis.

If you have any questions about your case please call me. I will be happy to speak with you and help you every way I can.

Brent Adams

APPENDIX

North Carolina Industrial Commission

IC File #_____

NOTICE OF ACCIDENT TO EMPLOYER AND CLAIM OF EMPLOYEE, REPRESENTATIVE, OR DEPENDENT (G.S. 97-22 THROUGH 24)

Emp. Code #_____

Carrier Code #_____

Employer FEIN_____

The I C. File # is the unique identifier for this injury. It will be provided by return letter and is to be referenced in all future correspondence

The Use Of This Form Is Required Under The Provisions of The Workers' Compensation Act

James Bob Baker				Triangle Loading		(919) 765-4321
Employee's Name				Employer's Name		Telephone Number
123 Middle Road				444 Hipex Avenue	Dunn	NC 28910
Address				Employer's Address	City	State Zip
Apex	NC	27616		Nation's Mutual		
City	State	Zip		Insurance Carrier		
(919) 123-4567		(919) 765-4321				
Home Telephone		Work Telephone				
xxx-xx-1234	☒ M ☐ F	04/09/68				
Social Security Number	Sex	Date of Birth				

EMPLOYEE – This form must be filed with the Industrial Commission within two years of the date of injury or occupational disease or your claim may be barred. Notice shall be given to the employer as soon as the accident occurred or as soon thereafter as practicable and within 30 days. (This form should also be used for occupational disease claims; however, for asbestosis, silicosis and byssinosis, Form 18B is to be used.)

Notice is hereby given, as required by law, that the above-named employee sustained an injury or contracted an occupational disease, described as follows: __08:23__ ☒ A.M. ☐ P.M. on __01/11/07__ at __Dunn, Harnett__ Describe the injury or occupational disease,
Time of Injury   Date (Required)   City and County
including the specific body part involved (e.g., right hand, left hand) __Right leg__
Describe how the injury or occupational disease occurred: __Broke leg when fell off of loading dock while loading freight__

Occupation when injured: __Loading Technician__ Nature of employer's business: __Trucking Company__

Disability began: __01/11/07__ Return to work date or period of estimated disability: __00/00/00 or Undetermined__
Date   Date   Period

Weekly wage: __$1200.00__ Number of hours worked per day: __8__ Days worked per week: __5__

EMPLOYER: This notice is being sent to you in compliance with requirements of the North Carolina Workers' Compensation Act, in order that the medical services prescribed by the Act may be obtained; and, if disability extends beyond 7 days duration, or if death ensues, compensation may be paid according to law.

(signature) _____ (910) 555-5555
Signature (Check One) ☐ Employee, ☒ Attorney,   Telephone Number
☑ Representative, or ☐ Dependent

P.O. Box 1389   Raleigh   NC   27546   06/08/07
Address   City   State   Zip   Date Completed

NOTE –If injured is unable to sign this, another may sign for him. This form should be typewritten if possible. Employee should retain one signed copy of this notice, mail one signed copy to Industrial Commission at the address below, and furnish employer with one signed copy.

For IC use ONLY	
Nature_____	
Body_____	
Cause_____	
SIC_____	
Coder_____	

FORM 18
5/01
PAGE 1 OF 1

FORM 18

MAIL TO:
NCIC - STATISTICS SECTION
4334 MAIL SERVICE CENTER
RALEIGH, NORTH CAROLINA 27699-4334
MAIN TELEPHONE: (919) 807-2500
OMBUDSMAN: (800) 688-8349

◆

WORKERS' COMPENSATION IN NORTH CAROLINA

North Carolina Industrial Commission

REQUEST THAT CLAIM BE ASSIGNED FOR HEARING

IC File # _____
Emp. Code # _____
Carrier Code # _____
Carrier File # _____
Employer FEIN _____

The Use Of This Form Is Required Under The Provisions Of The Workers' Compensation Act

James Bob Baker
Employee's Name
123 Middle Road
Address
Apex   N.C. 27616
City   State   Zip
919-123-4567   919-765-4321
Home Telephone   Work Telephone
XXX-XX-1234 ☒M ☐F 4/9/1968
Social Security Number Sex Date of Birth

Triangle Loading   919-765-4321
Employer's Name   Telephone Number
444 Hipex Avenue Dunn NC 28910
Employer's Address   City State Zip
Nation's Mutual   0000123
Insurance Carrier   Policy Number
111 Con Road Fayetteville NC 28823
Carrier's Address   City State Zip
252-111-1111   252-222-2222
Carrier's Telephone Number   Fax Number

I, Iam Taerg _____, respectfully notify you that the above named parties have failed to reach an agreement in regard to compensation, and I request a hearing.

We have been unable to agree because (state reason with specificity): Defendants have denied the claim via a Form 61.

Employee believes he or she is entitled to the following workers' compensation benefits (check all that apply):

☒ Payment of compensation for days missed (give dates): January 11, 2007 - present (ongoing)

☒ Payment of medical expenses/treatment: From date of injury - ongoing and future treatment.
☐ Payment for permanent partial disability:
☒ Payment for permanent and total disability: Not yet assigned
☐ Payment for scars:
☒ Other: Any education, training, or vocational assistance that may be needed in the future.

Has claimant participated in mediation? ☐Yes ☒No
Date of injury: January 11, 2007   Part of body: neck and back
City and county wherein injury occurred: Dunn, Harnett County
Estimated length of hearing: 2 ½ hours
Below is a list of names and addresses of all witnesses, including doctors, whose testimony is to be taken by the requesting party. Doctors outside the county of hearing are not required to attend this hearing.

NAME	ADDRESS
Betsy Johnson Regional Hospital (staff)	Dunn, N.C.
Dr. Fixme Nau	Dunn, N.C.
Dr. Kutem Goode	Raleigh, N.C.
Present and former employees of Def.	Fayetteville and Dunn, N.C.

MAIL TO:
NCIC - DOCKET SECTION
4336 MAIL SERVICE CENTER
RALEIGH, NC 27699-4336
MAIN TELEPHONE: (919) 807-2500
OMBUDSMAN.- (800) 688-8349

FORM 33
2/01
PAGE I OF 2   FORM 33

When a date of hearing is set, I respectfully request the Commission to send me signed subpoenas for my witnesses. When I receive these subpoenas, I will deliver them to the Sheriff of the county or counties in which each witness resides so that the subpoenas may be served.

Iam Taerg
(Signature of party requesting hearing, or attorney)

Attorney
(Title)

P.O. Box 1389 Raleigh, NC 27835
(Address: street and number, city, state and zip)

4/15/2007
(Date of notice)

CERTIFICATION

I, Iam Taerg hereby certify that this case is ready for hearing. This case will be set in the county where the injury occurred unless good reason is shown for a different location. If you want the hearing in a different county, name the county below and your reason for that location.

_____
(County)

_____
(Reason for setting)

Iam Taerg
(Signature)

Note: A copy of this form must be sent to opposing parties. The original of this form must be sent to the Industrial Commission at the address below:

MAIL TO:

FORM 33
2/01
PAGE 2 OF 2

FORM 33

NCIC - DOCKET SECTION
4336 MAIL SERVICE CENTER
RALEIGH, NC 27699-4336
MAIN TELEPHONE: (919) 807-2500
OMBUDSMAN.- (800) 688-8349

213

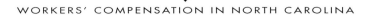

JOB SEARCH LOG

Date Applied: _____

☐ In-Person Interview
☐ Telephone Interview
☐ Submitted Resume'
☐ Other: _____

Name of Company/Business: _____

Name of Contact Person/Who I Spoke To: _____

Address: _____

Phone Number: _____

How I found out about this job: _____

Job Title: _____

Description of job duties: _____

_____

_____

Physical requirements for job: _____

_____

Educational requirements for job: _____

NOTES: _____

_____

_____

_____

_____

_____   _____
Signature of Interviewee   **Date**

FREE NEWSLETTERS
FROM BRENT ADAMS

Would you like some practical advice on how to deal with insurance companies?

Would you like to learn about interesting developments in the law that can affect your life?

Would you like to read the truth about the so-called "malpractice crisis"?

Would you like to learn how to protect you and your family when purchasing insurance?

These are some of the topics covered in a regular Newsletter sent to your home by North Carolina lawyer, Brent Adams.

Brent Adams believes that busy men and women benefit from taking a few moments out of their busy schedules to read a regular newsletter which gives basic information about legal issues likely to arise in their daily life. By having this information, the reader can be better prepared to deal with legal issues when they arise.

There is no cost or obligation to subscribe for this free newsletter.

If you do subscribe and later change your mind and decide you do not want to receive this Newsletter, you can call us toll free to cancel your subscription.

We try to make the information contained in this Newsletter interesting and useful.

To start receiving your free subscription on a regular basis, just photocopy this form, fill it out and mail or fax it to us. FAX to 910-892-0652 or mail to Brent Adams at PO Box 1389, Dunn, NC 28335.

Please start my subscription to your free Newsletter.

NAME:_____

ADDRESS:_____

_____

_____
      CITY   STATE   ZIP

DATE OF BIRTH:_____
WORK PHONE:_____
HOME PHONE:_____

If you would also like to receive our free E-Mail Newsletter, just give us your E-Mail Address. We do not share or give out to anyone our mailing lists or our E-Mail lists.

E-MAIL ADDRESS:_____